WIRES
UNTWISTING

Untangling the world of addictions

Sarina Wheatman

Michael Terence
Publishing

First published in paperback by
Michael Terence Publishing in 2019
www.mtp.agency

Copyright © 2019 Sarina Wheatman

Sarina Wheatman has asserted the right to be identified as the
author of this work in accordance with the
Copyright, Designs and Patents Act 1988

ISBN 9781913289287

No part of this publication may be reproduced, stored in a retrieval
system, or transmitted, in any form or by any means, electronic,
mechanical, photocopying, recording or otherwise, without the prior
permission of the publishers

Cover image
Copyright © Tawhy

Cover design
Copyright © 2019 Michael Terence Publishing

This book is dedicated to Olivia De Gruchy and friendship.
"The thing that is lost in everything I do"

Contents

About Sarina Wheatman i
Introduction iii
Forward vii
1: What is Addiction? 1
2: The Illness and the Solution 7
3: The Disease Concept 19
4: The Aliens Amongst Us 23
5: The Predator, the Conman and Me 31
6: The First Steps of redemption 37
7: Steps One to Three 49
8: Life as a Disaster Movie 61
9: Let's talk about alcohol 67
10: What to do to get well? 75
11: Recovery 81
12: Relapse 95
13: Anger and The Family 103
14: Secondary Care 109
15: Understanding Suicide and Addiction 113
16: Conclusion 117
Resources 119

About Sarina Wheatman

Having worked for many years as an addiction specialist, I hold the accreditation NCAC by The Federation on Alcohol and Drug Professionals (FDAP) as well as an accreditation by the Guild of Energists for Emotional Freedom Technique (EFT).

At the time of writing, I am employed by a clinic in Southampton. I also have a small private practice in Southampton. I am also blessed to have many years of continuing recovery myself. So, in my books, I talk about a method of treatment and recovery that I teach to patients as well as use myself. I have worked in a variety of treatment centres in the UK, the Channel Islands and Holland.

My first book, *Twisted Wires*, was written because I am constantly amazed at the ignorance of many people about the true nature of addiction. This ignorance leads to the stigma that is prevalent amongst society today. Most people coming to treatment feel an enormous sense of shame, for some this aspect of the disease keeps them away from seeking help. I would love to see a change in perception, hence the books.

The term *Twisted Wires* refers to the many crazy aspects of the disease of addiction, certainly the mindset of the addict could be viewed as illogical, but the twisted thinking extends outwards to just about everything associated with this Mental Health catastrophe.

Mental Health illnesses are at present 'enjoying' a more prominent position in the consciousness of our country, however, addiction continues to be the misunderstood sibling of all the illnesses.

My passion is to be part of a change of perception. My other passions include travelling and discovering new and exotic places, as well as the beautiful world of gemstones and gem collecting. In another life, I would train to be a geologist or jeweller. I love literature, of course, and find old bookshops and their contents thrilling and exciting. I can get lost in the worlds of make-believe as well as get very serious about my research and subject matter of my books.

Introduction

What is the point of another book about addictions and recovery? Isn't there enough information out there about the subject? You would think so, but there is still so much misunderstanding about this complex problem. Understanding about the disease comes slowly for most, certainly, with me, it has taken years and years. Years of clean and sober time, years of working in the field as an addiction specialist, years of study, asking and answering questions, research, delving into the questions and answers of other people's books and minds. It is a fascinating subject, this subject of the mind. No matter how much I learn, there is always more to discover. In this way, I keep my mind switched on. However, in all this interesting journeying it is important to remember that when it comes to addiction there are some tried and tested practical things addicts need to do to get and stay well.

Simple things, such as:

- **Abstinence from all mood-altering substances and or behaviours**
- **Admittance and acceptance that we cannot control these substances or behaviours**
- **Surrender to a belief that something can help**
- **Access that help**

- **Then continue doing the work on self to maintain a good attitude**
- **Practical ideas to change the way we think and respond**
- **We need to learn to live life on life's terms**

Simple to say perhaps, not so simple to do. This first three chapters will look at what addicts need to do to stay well. I will then introduce some personal anecdotes to describe some pertinent themes about recovery from my experience, and from the lives of some brave people who are willing to talk about their experiences of addiction and recovery. I shall introduce you to the concept of **'The aliens amongst us'** to highlight some perils that can befall the unwary in recovery.

This book is first to celebrate recovery because it is an amazing thing when somebody can reverse the downward trajectory of an out of control life of addiction. It's fabulous and worthy of celebrating, but there are many pitfalls and this book will examine some of them.

It will also introduce many other aspects of addiction that could or should be considered when travelling on this road to recovery.

My first book 'Twisted Wires' talked about how to find and access recovery, this book is more about what we addicts have to continue to do in recovery, or risk making mistakes, the worst, of course, is to not be aware of our thoughts and feelings and resume our substance or behaviour of choice, *just one more time*. 'Wires untwisting' refers to the tangled mess of unfathomable chaos (that is our brain, our thinking apparatus) which begins to heal and untwist when we stop using. The wires, twisted or untwisting, also refers to the many different aspects that surround addiction and recovery. The misinformation, the misunderstandings and the mistakes that recovery rooms are awash with. It seems that this world of recovery is filled with stories of relapses, destruction and sometimes death. The relapse rates are monstrously high. I suggest that some of this tragic circumstance lies in the attitudes that abound about this illness of addiction. I desire a change to this landscape. I lived in a mantle of shame and despair for many years with my own addiction, but I found a way out, I want the world to listen, take notice of a solution to the chaos and shame, and I want recovery to win. I also want everyone who is looking to find a solution to find their answers.

Forward

I first met Sarina twenty-seven years ago when she was in the process of training as an addiction counsellor, and I was being interviewed as a possible candidate for treatment at The Priory Hospital in Southampton. That was a lifetime ago.

This is Sarina's second book, the first 'Twisted Wires' tells of addiction in all its madness and proves the author capable of capturing the despair of both family and addict, supporting and informing them both with clarity. Sarina is a well known and respected professional in the field of addiction, treatment and recovery with a list of achievements to her credit. She has worked for many years with The Priory Group where she set up a programme in Jersey, a woman's group in Bournemouth and then researched the link between addiction and eating disorders back in Southampton. Later Sarina moved to Holland for a few years working in addictions and setting up aftercare facilities in Amsterdam and The Hague. Eventually, England beckoned her home where apart from a short stint helping ANA establish its residential programmes alongside her private practice, she was headhunted by The Manor Clinic.

Following my own treatment and rather colourful early recovery, I retrained as a psychotherapist. My apprenticeship as a rookie therapist began at long last and opened several doors. It was a miracle just as Sarina had told me it could be. I worked as a generic counsellor initially, then moved into addiction counselling. I set up a private practice, lectured on addiction, taught on counselling programmes and found my way onto several professional boards. Some of these focused on bringing professionalism to our field, others providing accreditation and support to addiction therapists. Eventually, I opened my own facility, ANA Treatment Centres, where the aim was to bring 'Treatment into The Real World' and provide excellent treatment for addictions whilst making it financially accessible to all. All that had been promised in recovery, if I chose to follow a few simple steps, has come to fruition, plus much more.

Let me now congratulate you on picking up this book. It is a book to inspire, to inform, to provide insight and to delight in recovery. It is a 'doing' book that moves us forward into a world where anything may happen if we are open to suggestions.

This book tells us of the writer's journey from a life of chaos, uncertainty and constant fear, to one of peace, acceptance and possibilities. This is a life told anew. Of the choices once robbed by addiction to the unfolding opportunities that present in recovery. At times this seems terrifying as does the realisation that we are responsible for ourselves.

We read of lessons learnt and of adjusting our grandiose ideas, learning to trust others, and how vital healthy relationships are to recovery. How important other people are to our wellbeing and sanity.

People often ask me do people truly recover[1] from addiction? I get the feeling some would like me to confirm their strongly held beliefs and reply no. But on the contrary, anyone can recover from an addiction if they really wish to. Yes, they need to address many issues honestly, not least the relationship they have with themselves. Recovery is open to all. As can be seen with the author's experience, the necessities are: faith, good support, willingness to listen, loss of ego and a good deal of love.

This book has been written with a good deal of love, with an appreciation for life and the many dear friends who have played a part in the author's story. They stand out for me as a reflection of the author's ability to return these friendships that form an on-going circle of recovery.

Libby Reid
NCAC[2] – Director, Founder & Chairman
ANA Treatment Centres

---

[1] Those of us in recovery do not use the word 'recovered' preferring to describe ourselves as being 'in recovery'.

[2] NCAC – National Counsellor Accreditation Certification.

1: What is Addiction?

To answer this question, it is perhaps easier to start with the things individuals become addicted to:

We begin with **alcohol** because it is the most easily accessible, it is legal and cheap, it has become part of life for many. It is available in most homes, supermarkets, corner shops, garages. It is used for celebrations such as weddings and our babies birth. It is used for commiserations at funerals or to de-stress after a tough day at work. It is used for just about every 'event' In life, yet, there are medical journals which say if it were a substance discovered today it would be a class A drug, in other words, very dangerous and illegal. So how come in our sophisticated society, it is so easily accessible?

We now move to **illegal drugs**, cocaine, heroin, crack, ecstasy, the list goes on and on, the one-time legal highs have moved into this slot (thank goodness) simply because calling these things legal give them a benign feel.

There is a whole mess of problems with the illegal status of drugs because it means users become criminalised if they use them. Yes, they need to be tightly controlled, but the use of them should not mean instant criminality.

In some countries, of course, people are put to death, or put in prison, or given 60 lashes if found with a prohibited substance. Our society then could be worse than it is. I would like it, however, to be better, which it will never be if the status quo remains as it is. The status of **marijuana** became confused, simply because it was de-classified, moved from a class A drug to a class B. The classifications depict the seriousness of the 'crime' when caught in possession of it. There was little explanation to this event so many just assume it is a "soft option" in the drug game. Many think it is "non-addictive." This type of thinking can be refuted as we witness long term smokers try to wean themselves off the drug. Most weed smokers I have met and treated have had horrendous problems trying to remain abstinent, experiencing all kinds of emotional and sometimes physical symptoms. This is not a 'soft' drug and can sometimes trigger psychosis in the unlucky.

Then there are **Prescribed medications,** some of the things GP's routinely prescribe can be addictive for certain people. **Chemists** also have a whole range of things that are addictive but easily obtainable. Opioids and sedatives being the ones that most easily spring to mind. It is not to apportion blame to Doctors or Chemists, but to state how easy it is to access some mind-altering chemicals. All these mood-altering substances can create havoc for people, so it is very interesting to ask why only a certain class of drug is illegal. I will reference material at the end of this book that delves into this question.

Behaviours can also become problematic for some, gambling, internet addiction, gaming, pornography, sexual compulsions, relationships, eating disorders which are, anorexia, bulimia and over-eating, spending/shopping, exercise addiction, cosmetic surgery and again the list is endless. Rehabs have been treating individuals with some of these problems for years, yet in the main, they are still not regarded or seen as addictions.

Then in almost a separate list, we have nicotine, sugar, energy drinks, caffeine and again the list goes on.

Some of the things on the list could be viewed as more desirable to have as a problem. **Caffeine - sugar? Really?** As more research is conducted, more warnings are appearing about some of these things, after all, it was not so long ago that nicotine was accepted and feted as a sophisticated addendum to anyone's image. It is laughable now of course as the dangers are well understood yet addicts still smoke and nicotine is easily available to all. The strange thing is that with many of the illegal substance around today, once upon a time they were easily available too and used in mainstream life by some people, just like nicotine. If you care to research some of the history and attitudes surrounding most of these substances you will discover a fascinating story. With all the substances and behaviours, some people can engage in their use with impunity and some become hopelessly addicted. Some can take it or leave it, others cannot leave it alone. Confusing and baffling, dangerous and deadly. I advocate for strong regulations, and of course for the illegal trade in all drugs to be controlled, but an overhaul in how we view people who simply 'use' should really be implemented.

Internet Addiction

I must talk a little about the newest game in town, or rather internet and gaming addictions. It is still a relatively new area, but it is most definitely 'a thing'. Having worked with several youths in Holland who were addicted to War and Fantasy games, I know that the resulting problems resemble many other addictions in existence. They play to the exclusion of everything else. Life becomes reduced to a bedroom and computer screen. Their education and family life are affected, all that matters is another level of the game they are playing. These young people became basically loners, the only acquaintances they want are other gamers they meet online. The heartbreak of families watching their children's lives fall apart in front of their eyes is something I cannot forget. Yet again in this area of Mental Health issues, there are the naysayers that do not believe gaming fits the classification for addiction. The diagnostic criteria are to be fair, under review, but the parallels between the classical problems of drug addiction and alcoholism, and these behaviours are remarkably similar.

Internet Addiction:

"Internet addiction is a behavioural problem that has gained increasing scientific recognition in the last decade, with some researchers claiming it is a "21st Century epidemic" The classification of Internet addiction has been problematic ever since the terms conception in the mid-1990's. In an effort to provide consensus and clarity in this area, the American Psychiatric Association (APA)

proposed the inclusion of Internet Gaming Disorder in the revised fifth edition of the Diagnostic and Statistical Manual for Mental Disorders (DSM – 5), although this has led to greater confusion as Internet Gaming Disorder is arguably a sub-type of Internet addiction and/or a sub-type of video game addiction."

— Daria J. Kuss and Mark D. Griffiths
Internet Addiction in Psychotherapy

What is Addiction?

(Shush here comes the science bit!)

The "Diagnostic and Statistical Manual of Mental Disorders, Fifth Edition," often called the DSM-V or DSM-5, is the latest version of the Psychiatric Associations gold standard text on the names, symptoms, and diagnostic features of every recognised mental illness – including addiction.

The DSM-V criteria for substance use disorders are based on decades of research and clinical knowledge.

What are Substance Use Disorders?

The DSM-V recognises substance-related disorders resulting from the use of 10 separate classes of drugs: alcohol; caffeine; cannabis; hallucinogens (phencyclidine or similarly acting arylcyclohexylamines, and other hallucinogens, such as LSD); inhalants; opioids; sedatives; hypnotics; stimulants (including amphetamine-type substances, cocaine and other stimulants); tobacco; and other or unknown substances. Therefore, while some major groupings of psychoactive substances are specifically identified, the use of other or unknown substances can also form the basis of a substance-related or addictive disorder.

*This information can be found at **www.verywellmind.com** written by Elizabeth Hartney PhD*

2: The Illness and the Solution

I have been sober now for more years than I ever drank or used mind-numbing chemicals. Is life better? I often ponder that question, and the truth is, that sometimes it is, and sometimes life just sucks, and I would give anything to numb it out for just a while. Is life better? The million-dollar question. I am not a stupid person so, of course, my answer must be yes, I could not go on putting the effort into sobriety if it were not. But at times, the truth is I do not want to look at the question or formulate an answer.

Of course, it must be better, otherwise, I would still be falling in and out of dangerous, crazy situations, partying in loud noisy places, trying to ensure that the blackouts that cursed all my drinking and using years did not arrive too soon. In trying to remember what it was that I saw in the getting high and wasted states is peculiar. I certainly don't see the attraction any more. Perhaps this is why I choose sobriety today. Yet for many years, getting high was all I wanted to do. I remember it today as a rollercoaster ride, a slow drive for an interminable time with a crashing roaring speeding finale. Every time, especially in the latter years of my usage, the out of control rollercoaster was the feeling I was left with. The sickness, coupled with physical ailments continued to pile up, so that the mornings after the night before, where the only thing I could think about was my sick retching frame, the struggle to return to a normal state took longer and longer, then when it came, the shame that accompanied 'normality' was so huge that I just wanted the blackout that I feared so much to put an end to my remembering. An example of this can be seen in the following short embarrassing tale.

At the time of this story, I was working on a ship crossing the channel. In port and off duty, I and some companions went to the usual drinking establishment as was the custom. Nothing out of the ordinary occurred for most of the night, however, I blacked out and the next thing I became aware of was 'coming to' on a Norwegian Vessel as it was preparing to leave the harbour. I had apparently made friends with the captain and was about set sail with him, happily, nothing else had happened, and I exited this ship pronto. I do however have chills when I remember this story today. I was lucky nothing worse than humiliation happened because of this blackout, but the shame at the time was enormous. I crawled home to nurse my hangover, telling myself "I would never go to that bar again". Please note the bar is the problem, not my drinking!

Easy to see perhaps how so many of the participants who live this kind of life, the countless addicts and/or alcoholics, end up wanting to die. The death element perhaps is not so much the goal, but just the price willing to be paid for the end of the pain. The endless repeat, this continuing to do the same thing time and time again which can only be described as insanity. "AM I MAD?" is the scream offered up to the universe. This question is asked in many ways at many different times in the life of an addict. A question without an answer, because of course, there is only the muddled mind of the addict in play. The behaviour looks mad, the feelings feel mad, and certainly, the thinking is mad. The only solution when in the throes of serious addiction is to have another, drink, pill, substance or whatever. To use again is the only thing that soothes the addled feelings and mind. In the end, addicts all crave an end to the insanity and the pain it brings. So, if not death, then certainly there develops a sense that something must change.

It is hard to fathom now in my sober state of mind, why or how I could not see or stop this destructive pattern. The truth of this is, that at the start of each ride, each binge, the end result was never contemplated. The build-up of excitement as the ride was initiated, the feelings that the substance promised of euphoria was the thing that was so appealing. This time, it would not get out of control, this time, it would not go wrong. However, when it did, time after time it seemed it was the price I was willing to pay, no matter what the consequences. This is the bizarre state that millions of people with the illness of addictions go through time after time. In the hours before or after each 'event', addicts take on an outwardly sane, normal appearance. Life looks normal, a job, a home, relationships all things that many humans desire are possible for a time. But as the rollercoaster begins to speed up, and the substances or behaviour are used more frequently, it grows more and more impossible to appear normal. It is at this time that the companions, friends and loved ones of the addict notice, get angry or pull away.

This certainly occurred in my life. The people in my life seemed to care for me, so it appeared that my apparent craziness was a price they were willing to endure. Endurance, however, is never a good thing for relationships, and eventually, even the people who loved me would have to pull away, leave me or I would leave them before they tried to stop it all. I would always run before they did, left jobs before I got dismissed, and changed countries because a geographical was easier than facing the truth about myself. 'Truth' they say will 'set you free', and most certainly for the addicted person only the ability to see self as one really is, can break this destructive cycle. This breaking through of denial happens differently for everyone, it is sometimes a sharp shocking event for some, but for me, it was a gradual awareness that I was not living the kind of life I should or wanted, that I was not the kind of person I ever envisioned myself to be. In my sober state, I despised the me I became when I used. Eventually, of course, I despised myself continually. I became miserable, depressed and ashamed of myself and my life, I had to do something.

Once this awareness had been gained it appears that I had reached what is known as my 'rock bottom' I was in a place that felt so terrible, lonely and terrifying that I was prepared to do just about anything to change this landscape. The stars aligned, the wheels clicked into place and in the spinning wheels of fate, my cry of despair was heard, and a solution was reached. Did it come from me, did I decide, or was there something bigger directing events? Some say it is a God thing, some say it was determination, some say it was common sense or fate, I say, "does it even really matter?" What matters is that because of the rock bottom a sick desperate woman walks into a meeting with other recovering addicts and in the one and a half hours she was there walks out never to use mind-altering chemicals again. This I see as a miracle, I see it today as such, because how is it possible, that after years of destructive addictive behaviour, suddenly my life turned around and began a metamorphosis? These recovery miracles occur repeatedly in millions of lives, people who were once deemed hopeless find a solution.

We should really be investigating this phenomenon; our best scientific minds or doctors should really be shouting it from the treetops. Instead, the solution is largely ignored or derided. Only a very small number of people with addictions find this solution. Even though the statistics for the disease are catastrophic, even though more and more research is occurring about this disease, the 12-step, abstinence-based solution, is largely ignored. Who, for instance, understands that it is not a choice, but rather a *disease of choice*. A brilliant explanation of this can be found in **Kevin Macauley's DVD, Pleasure Unwoven**, he explains it as a problem of 'flawed thinking', that there are genetic components to this illness that are activated by usage. It is a primary illness, a chronic and progressive illness and ultimately, of course, a fatal illness. It is possible to get better, but abstinence completely and forever is the only way.

Abstinence is the key and the biggest sticking point for every addict, as the obsession for every addict is to use normally, many think that with a few months of clean time it proves "I am cured" The addicted person must learn that 'the first use of a mind-altering substance does the damage.' They must be reminded that this fact is true forever, it will be a lifelong task to maintain abstinence, and if mind-altering substances are used again they will risk sinking back into abject misery and re-connecting with a life of destruction. Once addicts have crossed those invisible lines into addictive use, they can never go back to 'normal' again. In recovery, the illness must be kept dormant and inactive. There are many things a recovering person must be mindful of in keeping the illness dormant.

Sleeping Tiger

Addiction in its dormant phase can be described as a sleeping tiger, if it remains curled up and asleep, the problems do not reoccur, however, once this tiger begins to purr, sit up and stretch it usually means trouble is on the way. Many things can make the tiger active again and it is this the newly sober alcoholic or addict needs to learn. If the tiger is not quickly subdued the individual will begin to feel restless, irritable and discontent and craving relief will not be too far away, and once this state has been reached, a return to the substance or behaviour of choice is almost inevitable. A relapse can be averted, but it is difficult at this stage, much better not to wake that dammed cat!

Some examples of things that do awaken the tiger are; going to 'wet' place's and mixing with 'risky' people. Re-engaging with old using friends. Missing recovery meetings. Late nights, no timetable, no structure. Not eating correctly. Keeping thoughts and feelings a secret. In fact, a return to all the behaviours that recovery attempts to correct. All these things would indicate that the old ways of thinking have come back, and our greatest problem is flawed thinking!

The problem now and for always can be understood as flawed thinking. It is this that addicts need help with even after the using has ceased. But it is exactly this that is largely misunderstood even by addicts themselves, but also certainly by their loved ones and society at large. That substances or compulsive behaviours no matter what they are can create mayhem in a person's life is perhaps understood. That the faulty crazy thinking that contributed to the problems in the first place can remain when abstinent, is perhaps not so well understood. The using of the substance is, after all, only another symptom of what is really wrong with addicts.

So, What is Addiction?

"A reliance on a substance or behaviour in order to change the way I feel"

The Solution to Addiction?

Starts with abstinence, born out of desperation and despair. Perhaps it is easy to understand why everyone imagines that simply stopping the substance or behaviour that seems to be causing the problems is the only thing that needs to happen. But this is to totally misunderstand what is wrong with people who become addicted.

The problem is the way addicts think. They have flawed thinking, insane thinking, with a brain that triggers a craving for a substance or behaviour that destroys them. There is no way to stop it once they have crossed the unseen, unknown lines that depict addiction. Until they realise what is happening and want to stop it, only then are they able to seek and receive the help that they need. Help will always begin with abstinence. It generally takes years for the progression of the illness to create the need or want to stop. Only the lucky few find solutions to this illness early in the disease. Usually when the realization comes it is too late or too difficult to stop alone, if at all.

Let's Talk About the Brain

It has been mainstream knowledge for some years that addiction begins when the brain's pleasure centre repeatedly experiences an abnormal build-up of a chemical called dopamine. A rise in dopamine levels are also created when doing normal things like eating, having sex or taking part in recreational activities. Consumption of drugs and or alcohol and medications can also boost the brains dopamine levels, but in a far more powerful way. This means that for some people who start to use drugs and alcohol they will fall into patterns of repeated behaviours, with the using becoming excessive. They want to re-create the strong pleasure sensation they experience. Then over time, the way the brain produces these chemicals changes. The addict relies on continued use of the substances to feel 'normal' and will crave the substances to achieve or chase the euphoric feeling again. There is a whole raft of other things that occur but essentially this insult to the brain on a continuous basis creates stress and distress which in turn can create all kinds of health-related problems. The pleasure or reward symptom is so strong however that the addict, not really understanding any of this process in the brain, will go on using the thing that creates the dopamine spikes until some of the 'trouble' as described in later chapters starts to highlight there is something very wrong.

Addiction is confusing because not everyone reacts to drugs and alcohol in the same way. In some families there is not always a 'pattern' of behaviour, it sometimes skips generations, and in other families, everyone in the family is affected. So, no pattern exists to warn of possible addictions, or to predict there will problems going forward if you use. Repairing the damage done to the brain takes abstinence and persistence in providing the body and brain with an alternative way of living. Low mood, distress and depression are common states at the start of any recovery. Time is the great healer, but addicts need to do very much more to heal and stay healed. **Addiction** is not a question of a failure of will or strength of character or morals, as is often thought. Research contradicts this notion.

Much of the bad press about addiction occurs because it looks so self-indulgent. "Why can't they just stop?" is a refrain said hundreds of times by anyone contemplating the crazy actions of the out of control addict. So many broken promises and so many lies occur in the life of a practising addict, that it is sometimes very difficult to have sympathy for this illness. Yet for many addicts, once they discover the theory about the disease concept and can accept it, they will go on to recover and lead productive lives free from the chains of addiction. This illness is like no other. No other illness creates so much anger, contempt and arguments about its origins. The addicts themselves do not want to admit to having it, they will go on denying it despite drastic and devastating consequences until there is no place left to hide and no-one left to believe the lies. If the hapless addict's brain is still somewhat intact it is usually at this point something could penetrate the thinking and elicit the changes needed for recovery.

So this is the good news about recovery, the addictive pathways that are created in our brains during the active using phase can restructure in time. But time is the thing addicts sometimes are not patient with. Feeling better NOW is an often-heard refrain. If addicts could understand a little about how the brain works, what it takes to create the addiction and what it takes to change it all again, perhaps patience would be easier to access.

Addiction changes the brains communication pathways. Creating new paths are difficult and a slow process. We need help to do it. Patience to achieve it. But first, we must believe it. To begin to believe it, research is the answer.

Research that involves *addiction and the brain*, neuroscience is the new buzzword, but explains such a lot that previously was confusing. There will be some references at the end of this book to help point you in the right direction.

3: The Disease Concept

Disease Concept definition – '*A reliance on a substance or behaviour to change the way I feel*'

Addiction – *Recognised as a disease by The World Health Organisation, The Medical Association and many other august bodies.*

It is most assuredly time to stop arguing about," *is it or is it not an illness*?" If everyone could agree on the diagnosis, perhaps we could get on with the job of educating and treating people who have this disease, and /or educating everyone else so that they do not fall into its trap, or if already in it more easily find a way out.

However, to go back to the original question, is life better in recovery? Of course, without my sick addict behaviour that infects and affects everything around it, life itself becomes better. Am I better? In many ways, I feel just the same. I know I am not, having let go of much of the selfish, self-seeking behaviour which is so usual in addiction, my behaviour has vastly improved. With improved behaviour, comes improved life circumstances. For years things continued to get better, however, I will attempt to explain what can go wrong for even the most 'sober' of people. I will attempt to explain how I, with many years of clean and sober time under my belt made a series of catastrophic decisions, which ultimately led to some dire circumstances in my life, and which cause me to really question 'Is life better?' I hope to show how even as our 'twisted thinking' improves with sobriety we are still capable of becoming tangled in those twisted wires which are so hard to understand and keep untangled. I hope to show how the 'aliens amongst us' the people who live amongst all of us, largely unseen and hidden, can strike the unwary, and perhaps I will explain how to avoid making these same mistakes, or at the very least learn to navigate around them.

Aliens – belonging to a different country, race, group or species.

Everyone assumes that the only thing that needs to occur in the alcoholics/addict's lives is the will- power to stop using. If the using stops then the bad behaviour or the dangerous practices will stop. Yes and no, the using must stop, abstinence needs to be achieved, but to assume that the problems stop when the using stops is foolhardy or naïve. What is required is a complete overhaul in the addict's life. There are patterns of thinking, behaviour and attitudes that need to be examined and, in some cases, changed. This is impossible to do by oneself… One of the first things an addict who goes to a 12-step group learns is that they are 'powerless' over their drug of choice, if they could have found a solution by themselves they would have already done so. The going along to a meeting or going to a rehab, or counselling is already an acknowledgement that the answer was not found. A complete overhaul in the addict's life will be impossible to achieve if the only thing to happen was that the using stops. It is, of course, an important start in any recovery story, but, sometimes abstinence creates a whole new set of circumstances that result in pain, depression, more bad behaviour and, in extreme cases, suicide. The brain that is wired differently has come to rely on a substance to change the way feelings are felt and processed. If the brain could be seen more like a computer system that needs re-booting or de-fragging, you would get more of an idea of the complex process that recovery from addiction requires.

This process is achieved by the person with addiction becoming involved in a recovery programme. The 12-step movement that was started in the USA is the most well-known and successful of systems around. Surviving despite much misinformation about it. Some of its concepts are taught in many treatment centres and rehabs, and of course is accessed by the individual going along to regular 12-step meetings. Any recovering person will attest to the need to continue this 'de-fragging' process through on-going participation in the meetings and involvement with other recovering people. There is also the tried and tested process of the 12-steps, these are the process through which people can make the changes necessary to stay well. They are simple statements with a wealth of meaning which require thought, time and other experienced people to really understand. The 12-step principals, which will be taught at the meetings, must be practised continually, and it is a mistake to assume one can be well just because the using has stopped. The legendary flawed thinking of the addict continues on lots of levels. The next chapter will recount a tale all about flawed thinking, and how the unwary can fall into decision making traps without really realising it.

In the following story, **resemblance to anyone living is purely coincidental, it is a fictionalised version of events.** However, the fact that there are predators amongst us is real and they reside in every town and village of our world, as well as in recovery communities. There are many similar stories that can be heard in recovery, this is just one of them.

4: The Aliens Amongst Us

In the following drama, the principal players are Silas the Snake, Billy the Weasel and Me.

The Predator - *predatory (adjective) hunting, raptorial, ruthlessly exploitive to others intending harm.*

Snake, *reptile, slithering, dangerous, cold, ruthless, lethal.*

Narcissistic – *self-love, self- adoration, self- obsessed egotistical.*

Silas the snake, loved adoration, he craved it and had learnt from a very young age how to get exactly what he wanted, from his mother, his siblings, from school friends, girls, boys and whomever he turned his charm on. He had always been handsome, and from his teenage years knew exactly how he could manipulate and use the unwary. He had not yet developed his more lethal traits, but was already showing signs of cruelty to others, which later would direct his more odious behaviours.

He was not content to live a little suburban life, with a family who, although gave him all that they could, was not enough for him, not rich enough, not smart enough and not worldly enough. Silas had plans, big plans and they did not include these people he lived with. Despite his mother's pleadings he departed for the big city and set about creating his new improved universe. He was charismatic when he wanted to be, realised it opened doors. Therefore, what Silas wanted he took, he charmed, and manipulated, he grew quite business savvy and the money, the people and the adoration he craved all flocked to him. There were golden years when all a man could desire was his. But as we are talking about addiction, the more he got, the more he wanted and what he had was never enough. As his craving for money, sex, power and illicit substances grew, his once striking visage began to lose its appeal. It began to show avarice and greed, a lust that could not be satisfied. He had never learned what must be learned in life, that true beauty and contentment comes from within, and of course, includes how the world and its inhabitants are treated. His behaviour in the world created ugliness. He squandered his talents and his beauty, and as the years passed it could all be seen in the ravages on his once lovely face. He had the cunning of all addicts who are out of control, he knew how to conceal, how to use smoke and mirrors and was still able to reel the unsuspecting into his web.

In his world he kept the more powerful close, he put on a mantle of respectability and of generosity, he gave to worthy causes, as long of course as it served to elevate his position. No-one in his inner circle suspected a thing. There were murmurs, of course, a few hurt and angry people who were brave enough to speak out, but his victims were chosen for their vulnerability. They did not have a voice to be listened to, nobody listened to what they said, and because of this, his behaviour escaped attracting attention from anyone who could have stopped him. He became more cunning, more powerful and more corrupt. Along with his addiction to substances came many more obsessive cravings, he loved sex but as this addiction developed so did his need for more and more experiences that he sometimes suspected were wrong, so he grew more secretive. It seemed he had no limits, no care for his conquests, and seemingly no morals. Silas had become over the years a creature of the dark, a slithering dangerous predator, who preyed on the unwary and innocent.

To be continued........

The Conman – *illusionist, deceiver, liar, deliberate attempt to deceive.*

Weasel – *Mammal, sly, quick, hunter of weaker prey.*

Billy was a weasel, he looked like a weasel, he sounded like a weasel, small and pinched with an air of scrabbling around from place to place. If he didn't want to be noticed, he had the ability to blend into the scenery. He ran arms between countries, on a small scale you understand, no big-time corrupt businessman here, corrupt yes but strictly small time. He messed up hugely on one deal and had to leave his hometown under threat from the local kingpin. When he told the tale, he laughingly said he didn't want to be kneecapped, as though this proved what a ferocious 'gangster' he was.

No, Billy was anything other than dangerous, or ferocious or successful. But he developed an air of cunning and an ability to look for the next best thing. An ability to talk his way out of trouble or to talk his way into someone's confidence. Initially, he was always believable, and it was his innate ability to be convincing that made him such a good conman. He spent much of his youth wandering around Europe brokering small deals, some of which netted him a good profit. He had relationships of course, but nothing lasted, he could never keep his façade from slipping and in the end, his latest 'hostage' in the relationship games he played grew tired of his fabrications and left him to it. So, Billy was adrift, lonely, bored and needing something to occupy him. He decided that a good way to influence and ultimately get what he wanted from others, would be to have a profession.

It took some time and manipulation, but Billy re-created himself as a professional man, respected with all the right sounding credentials. If anyone had looked hard enough they would have uncovered some blazing inconsistencies with his training and qualifications, but remember the conman, the man who could get what he wanted and make others believe his lies and manipulations. Quite a skill really and had he been genuine could have been a force for good in the world, however, he was not genuine and so as is the case in all these affairs his skill was put to garnering himself exactly what he wanted.

What did Billy want? He wanted position and status and money. An easy life where it would be simple to get everything he wanted. He was tired of being one step ahead of the law, tired of avoiding trouble. He had always been small and pinched but as he aged this became more pronounced, and his stooped whiskery face became more weasel-like. He didn't look like a threat, and he sounded wonderfully caring, wonderfully knowledgeable, whomever he worked with believed him and trusted what he said. He did not look like a threat, but a threat he was, because Billy was always on the lookout for the main chance and his next victim. If you knew what you were looking at you would have described Billy as a sly creature, preying on the weak and the unwary.

Me – the Chameleon – blends into the environment – ability to change

Strong-willed – egotistical – stubborn and naïve or foolish

So how does someone like me become tangled up in the lives of two such men? I have my own stories of course but nothing like theirs, and really, I should never have collided with their universe at all. But fate has a way of rolling the dice of putting all the stars in place and one ping of the right or wrong button sets events in motion and hey presto here we are all together in one place.

But let me start a little before this moment. With hindsight now, I can piece this story together, I can see how and why it occurred. The purpose of telling this is to show how easily the twisted wires of the addict's mind can make mistakes that were never intended. Even the minds of long sober recovering people make mistakes if they do not work the programme. I have been substance-free for more years than I ever used mind-altering chemicals, but I forgot you see, that my thinking was/is flawed, if I don't continue to follow the tried and tested formula of the 12-step programme I will continue to make flawed decisions, and boy, the decisions I made were very flawed.

The story begins:

My long term living companion had just died, the grief was overwhelming, I did not think I would get over it, we all think like this, of course, this is the nature of grief, but moments passed into days, into weeks and I did get over it. I did survive although at times I wished I had not. Life took on a mechanical feel, one foot in front of the other, doing what had to be done to live and prosper. It seems understandable that my broken heart was then given another task to overcome, I developed a critical illness, breast cancer. I endured many months of surgery, chemo, radiotherapy and was very very ill. The doctors and nurses looking after me were amazing and living near the best teaching hospital for cancer in the country meant that my chances of survival were amplified. I did survive but there was a huge cost to pay in terms of my view on life. Some people view their brush with death in this manner as a second chance at life, I was not so grateful. Outwardly I looked normal, inwardly I was empty and directionless. After the difficult months of recovery, when the company I worked for and had retained me during all of this difficult time offered me the chance of an early redundancy I imagined this was a sign for me to make changes, which is exactly what happened. Selling my house, and many of my possessions was painful but I told myself it had to be done, I had to free myself up and be ready for what life had in store for me next. Philosophical and practical I looked for opportunities on the internet, which is where I saw the advertisement for a job that interested me. I researched the name of the company's boss, he came up as impressive and successful, so I applied, went for the interviews and lo and behold got the job, and so voila, just like that Silas the snake and Billy the weasel entered my life. Just like that, I put into play a set of circumstances that were all my own doing. An advertisement on an internet screen. A broken heart looking to be mended, a life wanting something new. Well, new, was exactly what was on offer, and before too much thought had entered the equation, things were packed, sold, stored and ready and I set the plan in motion. I can understand today that because of the events just described, I was most likely in the throes of depression. I had counselling at the time, and all of my dear friends and family rallied around. I should have understood my state of mind a little better, especially with the type of work I do, however, nothing it seemed would stand in the way of creating a new life. It seemed exactly what I should do.

The 'wires' that had been so carefully and methodically untwisting were beginning to become quite twisted again.

The scene is set, the players are introduced, and the process of flawed thinking and its consequences resumes.

5: The Predator, the Conman and Me

Silas was odd looking these days, the allure of his younger years had long since been replaced. If you knew what you were looking at you could see the brutality and corruption in his eyes and ravaged face. He was careful however to conceal himself, a little like the vampires in popular culture, you never saw the danger until it was too late. He had the ability to create excitement when interacting with others, he was skilful with the way he manipulated, and this was the man I went to work for. He had the air of a successful entrepreneur, a benefactor and a man about town. To be around him was interesting, one imagined it was the start of something, 'what thing?', well anything.

That was his skill, people always felt on the verge of something when spending time with him. He always had an entourage of sweet young things around him doing his P.A., his typing, his accounts and sometimes doing nothing but making him coffee and tending to his needs. He was known around town, did local T.V. shows and was 'somebody', a big fish in a very small pond. The fact that he had a questionable past just added to his aura. To know Silas meant your days had potential. We all wanted to be part of it. So, if I, a well-seasoned woman of the world felt like this, then the younger more naïve subjects of his obsession had no ability to see through his behaviour and lies. For Silas liked his victims young, the younger the better. I guess that is why he got away with his actions for so long, the young and naïve did not see the warnings before he struck, and then when he did, just like the poisonous creature that he was, they did not know how to extract themselves from his venomous grasp. Of course, no-one saw any of this until much later, by which time he was already in jail, locked away in the dark where he belonged.

Billy, just like Silas, excelled in fooling the unwary. His skill was in casting his line and reeling you in. "it's in the way that I tell 'em" was his favourite saying. In my case, first and foremost he made me laugh. We could spend whole afternoons exploring the town, finding ridiculousness in quite ordinary things, a shop window full of prosthetic limbs, not funny of course but the signs accompanying them made out in broken English made us for some reason curl over with mirth. Why? I could not explain except, "it was in the way that he told 'em!" I laughed at his account of trekking across Europe when much younger ending up in jail over some mishap or other. His stories were always far-fetched and calamitous with whatever adventure he was in ending in disaster. Perhaps this should have served as a warning, however, if there were any pin-pricks of unease, it never lasted long enough to form into anything substantial.

He made me laugh and for heaven's sake isn't laughter what was needed after the horrendous last few years? As we strolled along this quaint old town, savouring the sights and sounds of the unfamiliar, stopping off for coffee, or browsing in one of the many beautiful old bookshops, what I did not yet realise was that Billy was reeling me in. There was nothing romantic in our budding friendship. He had other more exotic tastes in the romance department, and I was too damaged by my past to want to explore any romance. But a friendship began, quietly and lightly on the streets of a foreign town. When events imploded around Silas at the place we all worked, we had more than enough of working so close to the depths of our boss's murky world. The job that for both of us had held so much promise, had diminished to something neither of us wished to be associated with any longer. Silas's traits and habits were beginning to be visible. He was angry, arrogant and unpredictable. What had started as admiration for the man and his vision, was turning into active dislike. But what to do?

Two ex-pats in a foreign town. Neither of us wanting to return to the UK yet. The idea of our own business venture was born. Seamlessly and with apparent naturalness the plan took shape. We would open our own business. A different enough concept and venture to what was already in town. We believed that with our skills and knowledge it could be just what was needed. So just like that, we made it happen. On paper our plans looked bright and rosy, luck, however, was absent from our plans, it just so happened that the whole of Europe was headed for a major financial crisis and as this began to gather force, our fledgeling business began to crumble. The contracts and promises we had garnered evaporated. The atmosphere in our offices began to grow toxic with arguments and disagreements occurring daily. It became apparent that there was no meeting of minds or anything else. All my money was being ploughed into keeping us afloat and no money was coming in, until one day Billy upped and left. Just like that, he fled back to England saying he couldn't cope any more. He would send me money, he would see me right. He never did.

These events were like little explosions going off in my life. I had never mastered the language of this country, I could just about make sense of the computerised paperwork and accounts that Billy had overseen. What became clear to me when he left was that I could not continue running this business. I was facing mountainous tax bills, rent and accountancy bills. I was sinking fast, terrified and alone and realising that this predicament was of my own making, my flawed thinking, my absurd ideas that I could make something work that had no solid foundation. This was different from my rock bottom at the end of my using substances. Different, but equally devastating and terrible. I couldn't even plead insanity due to addiction, or could I?

And this is the reason for telling you this sorry tale. My predicament was most definitely caused because of the disease. 'How come?' everyone says, 'she has years and years of sobriety, can this be caused through the illness of addiction too?' Let me try to explain, and perhaps my explanation will save you from any similar follies. But just to finish this story. After a monumental struggle to make everything work I finally realised I was beaten, I returned to England, as facing life penniless in a foreign town was much too frightening. The problem with my finances had continued to worsen to the point of bankruptcy. I return to England, lodge with friends, and settle for an Individual Voluntary Arrangement (IVA), the system that is one step better than Bankruptcy, not much better, but I am managed, my debts are managed and eventually paid. I am left to wonder how did this happen, how has my life come to this? and of course, that question from the beginning of this story, is life better in sobriety?

The next chapter will attempt to explain what must occur in the addict's life to protect them from their crazy flawed thinking. Not just at the start of recovery but always. This is the single most misunderstood thing in the whole misunderstood subject of addiction, and what causes the many relapses that we read about, and the disasters such as described in this chapter with the predator, the conman and me.

To say I was being 'assaulted' on all levels by life would be an understatement. I am eternally grateful that I did not relapse, I could quite conceivably have done so and perhaps could have persuaded myself that It was understandable. But thankfully I had learned many years previously that nothing, **no single thing that can occur in my life is a reason to use mind-altering chemicals for recreation or solace**. I understood early on in my recovery that a substance no matter how enticing its euphoric recall could be, could not, would not make any single event better or soften the blow of a disaster such as described previously. I know this with every fibre of my being, and up until today, it has kept me safe from the perils of relapse. For this I can be truly grateful, what I am not safe from though is the predicament that my flawed thinking led me into. It was not done with malice on my part of course and perhaps my state of mind at the start of the story is another excuse, but my inability to really use the programme of recovery that I always say I live my life by has created very difficult circumstances that continue to be far-reaching.

6: The First Steps of redemption

My first book 'Twisted Wires' talks about how to find recovery, it describes recovery as a series of small and big changes that need to occur in a person's behaviour and life to elicit change. These changes begin with understanding that the mind and thinking of an addict can be viewed as 'flawed' and to address this flawed thinking the addict needs to engage in therapy through attending AA meetings or seeing a counsellor or going into rehab or all these things. In most rehabs, amongst other life lessons the focus will be on the first three steps of a twelve-step process, not because the other nine steps are not important but because if the first three steps are understood it will enable the individual in treatment to establish themselves in the recovery world outside of treatment and hopefully find the help needed to complete the further steps.

First, however, the little matter of 'The Disease Concept' needs to be explained, understood and accepted.

The Disease Concept

'A reliance on a substance or behaviour to change the way I feel'.

This definition explains on many levels why addicts do what they do. Why they do it and keep doing it despite sometimes catastrophic consequences is the subject of much debate. The addiction question cannot easily be explained. Some refuse to accept that this sequence of strange behaviours with a substance or behaviour at its conception can possibly be called an illness. Yet with the onset of brain imaging and extensive research which continue to throw up more explanations, it is possible today to understand things that have not always been possible to explain.

It was first described as an illness by the founders of Alcoholics Anonymous many years ago, when there was no such possibility of seeing into the brains of living patients. Since those days there have always been two camps, two views about what the problem with addicts and alcoholics could possibly be. We describe addiction as an illness with its own signs and symptoms. It is a **primary illness** and as such is not caused by anything else. A person can have what is known in the medical profession as a **dual diagnosis** where other illnesses such as depression and/or bipolar or anxiety problems exist side by side with the addiction. If this is the case then all the problems need attention, one will not cancel out the other as is sometimes thought, 'if I sort my depression out I won't have to drink so much' or something similar.

Addiction is also **Chronic,** it develops over a long period of time, as opposed to acute, like flu which is there and gone in days or weeks.

Addiction is **progressive,** the progression can be seen and charted when a person goes to treatment or goes to AA and remains sober, but as the illness is developing the progression is not something that is generally focused on. On the one hand, you have a society that refuses to acknowledge addiction as a disease and therefore symptoms that could be seen and dealt with early on are often ignored or missed. On the other hand, you have the addict who is in a state of denial, what is denial? Well, one of the best explanations of this state is 'sincerely believing our own lies' the addict is secretive and deceitful precisely because he/she does not wish to be stopped and cannot believe anything is wrong. The denial serves as a buffer against seeing the truth and as a protection from others disapproval.

The progression of the illness is generally only viewed when disaster comes calling. The subtler signs and symptoms would not be reasons to stop drinking or using. A blackout, or a hangover or missing work or school are signs that should be looked at early on but are generally seen as just aberrations and therefore not important. High tolerance and the legendary hard drinker are often seen as cool, being able to drink our companions 'under the table' a skill, but these things as well as hiding exactly how much or how often we use are all signs that something is not quite right in what we are choosing to do for fun or to socialise. The progression as I have already said is generally only noticed when something disastrous occurs, in one of the major life areas.

Family, Relationships, Social life, Law, Work/Finances, Health

The thing that forces many addicts to seek help is usually when something has happened in one of these areas of life and the consequences can no longer be hidden. It is usually serious and results in a loss of dignity or worse. Hiding these many transgressions becomes the normal response to yet another binge, it is when the hiding is no longer possible that individuals can sometimes ask for or be persuaded to get help.

Family and relationships – are usually the first to suffer negative consequences. The addict must create an alternative reality to fit in with family life, it works for a while but eventually falls apart when family members can no longer bear the lies and deceit that go into keeping the masquerade alive. There is no honesty in any relationship, the masks and deception must be kept tightly in place. Children become addendums to family life whereas they should come first. They get in the way, they hear and see things they should not. They become the next generation to have mental health issues.

Social life – this is a difficult area to view a developing problem as most people will tend to mix with like-minded people, and frequent places where the behaviour does not look out of place, or that they feel they fit in. Many activities are dropped or stopped because they do not fit the criteria for 'having fun' Addicts are hardly likely to go to places where they may face disapproval for the way they use. As the progression of the illness continues it is not unusual to find that most social activities have stopped, the addict becomes more and more isolated, preferring his or her own company to anything that may interfere or disapprove with what they want to do. This, in turn, makes the whole business of flawed thinking worse. "Solitary" is used as a punishment in the prison system, addicts routinely prefer to be alone, and the punishment is therefore experienced by everyone else, as the thinking that powers out of control behaviour gets more and more mad.

Work – tends to be protected at all costs, the addict must be careful and smart, they must fund their habits after all. All kinds of manipulative behaviours occur in the workplace to continue and/or mask the using. Drinking in toilets or sniffing cocaine on a cistern are not normal behaviours but will be done by someone whose habit has progressed to the point they can no longer wait to get home to use. Days off work, sick leave, what is the truth behind the perennial sicknote? But eventually jobs can be/will be lost, the money dries up – then what? The park bench view of the alcoholic is always used as the example that depicts alcoholism, yet the park bench person didn't start there, they ended there, and when the money runs out, and the people we depend on walk away, what exists for most addicts other than something similar? The other thing about park benches is they are sometimes much more sanitary than the sofa in our flats or homes, where addicts end up hiding their disgusting habits with a mantle of respectability.

The Law - there are many stories of addicts/alcoholics who have evaded being caught for drink or drug driving, and many who have been caught and prosecuted. This is a peculiar area in most addicts' lives for if they manage to find sobriety and deal with some of their transgressions this area often produces a large proportion of shame. Yet in the throes of the addiction woe betide anyone who tries to stop them driving. They will always convince themselves and anyone else around, that they are okay and in control. The buying of illegal substances is another area where addicts routinely break the law, with little thought unless caught. Trouble with or without violence goes hand in hand with an addict's progressively worsening problem. Domestic abuse, fights on a Saturday night, injuries and vandalism all can boast addiction as one of the reasons for its increase in our streets and in our homes. It is well documented that the 'larger louts' of football fame are derided as one of Britain's more shameful exports.

Health - is the area where the most damage can be seen the most often, although there is a huge risk of things not being seen until too late, as internal organs and damage to the brain cannot be easily observed. By the time an individual has visible signs of ill health because of substance abuse, the problem has most likely been going on for a long time. If luck is on their side and the using of the substance stops then maybe they can recover. But there is a tipping point in all the abuse to mind and body, where if taken too far there can be no recovery. Insanity, depravity, isolation and horror are the result of untreated addiction.

Other aspects regarding 'the disease concept'

There is a **genetic component** to the illness, and certain things need to be in place for the illness to develop, but when it does, there can be no going back; the well-known phrase in recovery is 'once an addict always an addict.' The substance abuse part is only one of the symptoms of the illness which has flawed thinking as the formidable driver in all the crazy decisions made.

We must learn that:

The brain, the thinking apparatus and its thinking processes will continue to garner faulty decisions long after the substance abuse or addictive behaviour stops. The only way to recover is to abstain (always), and to do this, addicts must find others that can help and guide, and then to use the help that is available. Not just at the start of the recovery journey, but *always*. When the 'always' card is played and understood, how can anybody still believe that calling addiction 'a disease' is a cop-out? Yet I still hear this word being bandied about by people who perhaps don't realise that continuous sobriety requires continuous commitment.

The Brain and Sobriety

Some of the behavioural issues in addiction show up in a variety of ways. Obsessive or compulsive behaviours exist without the taking of substances. Behavioural addictions also exist. There is also a state called 'dry drunk' which as the name implies manifests as self-defeating behaviours, which grow steadily worse. Behavioural addictions and the dry drunk syndrome are similar. Both require abstinence and the 12-step programme to heal in these areas.

Let's Talk About Behaviours

Sportsmen and women who are in training or at the top of their game are often dedicated and sometimes obsessive about their training and sport. We all celebrate the fantastic achievements. In no way can we criticize this type of behaviour. However, there have been instances with famous athletes who if they also use alcohol or drugs cannot keep control of their use. Other stories occur around high achievers whose addiction to substances only show when their high-profile careers stop. They no longer have the discipline to accompany their dedication. Or the brilliant musicians with hedonistic lives, whose careers start on a high and end in despair. To get to the top they have most likely been dedicated or obsessive. What is this to do with addiction?

I can be very obsessive about different things, the most pertinent at present is writing. When ideas are flowing I can sometimes catch myself doing similar sorts of things that I did in my substance abuse years, I burn the midnight oil, my head buzzing with information, I HAVE to write it out, I have to get the next chapter done, I have to research this or that. I forget to eat, I'm too wired to sleep. I'm excited, I love it. Nothing wrong in this we think. Well, nothing wrong until my work suffers the next day after the night before, or I get headaches and backaches from too long sitting working at the pc. Or I start to resent interruptions from friends, I ignore the phone, I don't go out, a familiar picture perhaps?

In recovery parlance, this is called unmanageability. When the normal parts of life become affected adversely by something I am doing. So, what is happening?

Not so difficult to understand that it is something to do with 'serotonin' and 'dopamine' and 'adrenalin' and 'neurotransmitters'. Chemicals that allow signal transmissions in the body, and therefore communication among nerve cells. Some types of behaviours can trigger abnormal rushes of all kinds of chemicals which affect our brain and the way we feel. The dedicated athlete who trains to within an inch of the next world record can be subject to big crashes in mood if not training. The adrenalin hit experienced by the artist on stage playing or singing to thousands is huge, but once alone in the tour bus or hotel, the emptiness can be devastating. There are lots of documented evidence of famous successful stars of the stage and screen who are also depressives and struggle when not performing. Many retired high achieving business people end up in rehab when the discipline of a working life halts. In my case even though, I in no way compare what I do to any of the previous examples, except in what can happen to the way I feel If I don't keep my 'obsessive' writing and accompanying behaviour under control. If I take it too far then I suffer. I can be like this with many things, not just writing, I can become obsessive about people, dieting, music, spending and shopping, social media. It seems I am an addict! I have an addictive personality, and obsessive behaviour happens if I get triggered. If the behaviour carries on for too long and is unchecked, then a return to drinking or drugging I believe, is not too far away. Behaviour triggers the feeling which triggers a craving which if ignored may wake the 'sleeping tiger' and end up in relapse.

Dry drunk:

When a person has had a period of sobriety and they use again, this is a relapse. The 'dry drunk' status occurs in an addict who has started to recover but then drops any kind of recovery programme so that the behaviours, feelings and attitudes which create much of the angst in the addict continue unchecked. It is usually a miserable state to be in and one where others may notice and remark on the behaviour long before the addict him or herself realises something is wrong.

Getting back to the athletes or musicians or high achieving business-people who do not even know they are addicts, well their obsessive behaviours can aid the progression of this disease. So, the stark shocking events that seem to come out of nowhere and are splashed across the newspapers, have been building perhaps for a long time, just unseen. This is another reason to dispute the naysayers who think addiction as an illness is a cop-out. Something goes wrong in the choice process of the brains function, this, with the chemical imbalances all combine to create the perfect storm for addiction to progress to an out of control state.

If the person with this 'out of control' behaviour realises and elects to have treatment or go to a 12-step fellowship then they will be introduced to the concept of 'The 12-steps' A set of principles, or instructions if you like, to aid a journey out of chaos.

7: Steps One to Three

Step One

We admitted we were powerless over _____
– that our lives became unmanageable

Step one essentially is the step of surrender, where all denial is stripped away, where all attempts to negotiate and bargain with the illness is recognised and stopped, where abstinence is accepted as the start of something different. The gap left in the middle of the sentence is where to insert any one of the manifestations of addiction.

Some people are cross-addicted which means that more than one addiction is present, some people have other illnesses like depression and anxiety or bi-polar disorder to contend with as well. All these things and more, are regularly viewed in treatment centres and in the rooms of Alcoholics Anonymous and the accompanying fellowships. All the manifestations of the illness must be stopped and or treated. Step one is a tough old step to negotiate, it is a simple sentence to read and understand but hard to put into practice. If Step one has been achieved the individual realises that they cannot recover by themselves, that they need help. They have started the "Surrender" process, which is so crucial to begin the recovery journey. They will have accepted and admitted they have a problem, and no longer believe they can recover alone.

Exercise One:

Think of the word 'Powerless' what does this mean to you, what does the word conjure up in your mind? Are you powerless over anything? Can you imagine what it feels like? Can you admit and accept the notion that YOU are powerless over an inanimate object?

This concept is what addicts are asked to accept if they are following the 12-step method of recovery. When they do, sometimes after monumental struggles they enter a 'surrender' state.

Exercise Two:

Think of the word 'Surrender', try the notion out for size, can you do it, admit it accept it? What does this state feel like? What am I accepting and admitting to? I cannot stop using on my own, every time I decide enough is enough or promise to stop, I fail. I need help. I stop trying to control, as the very idea of control infers that my using is not normal.

Helplessness, Despair, Anger, Fury, Rejection, Disbelief, Shame. These are some of the feelings addicts routinely go through before they reach acceptance. Could/can you do it?

Addicts usually can only surrender when there is enough compelling evidence which they gather by looking at their using lives.

For Instance:

- Are people still talking to us?
- Waking up next to someone whose name you don't know. The shame envelopes you as you slink away hoping not to be noticed
- Coming to from blackouts, trying to find out if the behaviour has been noticed. 'Did we have a good night?' or 'How did I get those bruises?'
- Who got hurt insulted or frightened by our behaviour?
- Stealing from your child's money box, meaning to return it but forgetting. Have the kids noticed?
- Taking from housekeeping, or the mortgage money, just to get the next fix and lying and manipulating to cover up
- Having huge debts after yet another loss in the betting shop or casino, or online game, and doing it again and again, because *'this time I will win'*
- Stealing alcohol from a supermarket, *'they'll never miss it after all'*
- Drinking alcohol secretly in someone's home and replacing it with water or tea, so it is not noticed
- Promises and lies and promises and lies and promises and lies, never-ending
- Driving under the influence of alcohol and drugs, boats and bikes as well as cars. Leaving the scene of accidents so's not to be breathalysed

- Domestic abuse, violence in street and home, accidents and illness
- 'Coming to' on a ship bound for a foreign port with a stranger

Rage and misery, depression and sadness, vile horrible behaviour all because the euphoric pull of an inanimate object is stronger than us.

These are just some of the things that can occur in an addict's life. All very compelling, but it is sometimes extraordinary how much of this must go on before sanity prevails. Before denial is obliterated, and the truth can no longer be avoided, it takes a lot, and it is never easy. Sometimes the consequences are much worse, of course, when waking up in a prison cell should be enough evidence for anyone, sometimes it is, sometimes not. Insanity. My particular insanity in this example of the ship in my story was not even close to the point where I was willing to stop the addiction, or even look at it.

Sophie R - Sobriety date 28/9/17 - STEP ONE

Whilst in active addiction, I desperately obsessed over being able to control my drinking and drug using. I so badly wanted to be one of those people who could enjoy the odd glass of wine with their friends, and to be able to drink 'normally'. But understanding what Step one is about showing me that I have complete inept ability to control any form of mind-altering substances. Once a drink or drug is in my system, the phenomenon of craving has been triggered and I am once again in a viscous cycle of battling my own head. My own crazy head where *'one is never enough'*. To achieve Step 1, I only had to look at the damage I had caused to everyone around me, and the damage I had caused to myself. After recounting the destruction that I had put my family through, and the physical effects on my body and mental health, I was able to see how much life-threatening danger I had subjected myself to. All because of a battle with a mental obsession. I had to stop fighting, because the truth of addiction is that it is not a battle. It is more powerful than me and there is no 'fighting' or 'beating' addiction. There is only surrendering to what you are and choosing to live your life differently. My disease is cunning, baffling and powerful, it continues to try to convince me that *'just one wouldn't hurt'*. I re-live the pain of my using to remind myself of what could happen again. It's called survival!

Step Two

Came to believe that a power greater than ourselves could restore us to sanity.

Most newcomers to the recovery world look at this step and immediately feel "oh no it's a religious thing" Most people must be convinced that although it was written by two guys who were religious, one does not have to be religious for the programme to work for them. For the bewildered sick newcomer who is looking for help, it simply acknowledges the fact that left to their own devices they cannot recover, Something or someone other than self must help. For most people who don't believe in religion, then the group in their rehab or people in the anonymous fellowships becomes the power greater. This thinking and adoption of a method of recovery is in no way disrespectful to the millions of people with faith, yet even in the case of believers the fact that it is necessary to have 'human' guides to help and instruct should not be too difficult a concept, as priests and elders play the same role in all religions. Perhaps another way to look at it is that we all need others to help translate the concepts of the programme we are trying to adopt.

We discover in Step one that we were powerless, if this is the case what or who has the power to help me?

The philosophy of the 12-step programmes is generally what works best. After all, this organisation has survived since its inception in the thirties. There has been no sponsorship, no government funding, no advertising, yet millions today have become well and freed from crippling addictions using the programme started by Alcoholics Anonymous. Not everyone gets well of course, but many do, yet the detractors of this way of getting well tend to focus on the failures rather than the successes. It is called a cult; a religious movement and the meetings are mocked by some uneducated people. Yet the truth of this way of getting well is that if you plug into the power, people power, god power, good orderly direction power, then lives that have been devastated by addiction can change. Does it really matter what it is? It is this that is so unfathomable in the world today, this is a proven solution for many hopeless addicts, why are we not celebrating it and encouraging our young or our sick to investigate? If step two is understood properly, i.e. that the power that is going to restore my sanity comes from outside of myself, then this is where recovery starts. After all, if addicts could do it themselves they surely would have in the face of all the damage their addiction's cause. Anyone living through any of the list of crazy events previously discussed can argue that something needs to restore some sanity to life. Once addicts realise they need help, then it is just might be possible to access the resources to restore this sanity.

Exercise One:

If I cannot stop using on my own, and I accept I need help, where should this help come from? Who or what can help? What is a Power Greater than myself, and what happens if I use this power? Am I insane? How can I tell if I am restored to Sanity? None of the answers to these and many more questions can be discovered alone. Asking someone else who may have the answers is a start to coming to believe that something other than my own resources is needed to help me.

Ben W - Sobriety date 03/11/17 – STEP TWO

Step two for me is about maintaining a sense of humility, that I cannot recover on my own. It is about realising that I am not alone, that when I put my faith in a power other than myself, I can be restored to sanity. I can be free from the crazy, chaotic and damaging thinking and behaviour that made my life so unmanageable.

Step Three

Made a decision to turn our will and our lives over to the care of God <u>as we understood him</u>

Another expression of alarm is usually uttered at the mention of G.O.D. Treatment Centres and people who have been sober for some time are quick to point out the 'as we understood him' is underlined in the step and is the important words in the sentence. Some people have a faith, there are many beliefs, just as there are many who do not believe. We talk rather of the power of the group, or good orderly direction, the power of the philosophy of the 12-step movement. It can be anything other than self. We stress it must be people who understand addiction as it is easy to go down wrong lanes in the pathways to sobriety, and if our loved ones could not help us when we were using why should they be able to help us now. They are perhaps better seen as our inspiration to stay clean, but not who we turn to for help with our addiction.

Other addicts or specialists in the world of addiction understand the flawed crazy thinking processes of the sick addict better than anyone. If this step is understood, it, and the previous two steps are what launch us into a new way of life. It requires the individual to acknowledge the sick thinking as well as crazy behaviour that propelled the addiction, it requires the individual to acknowledge they need help to make better decisions and it requires the individual to put this belief into practice by checking out our decisions and plans with others.

All basic and simple to understand perhaps. For those of us who have found sobriety, it is a revelation and wonderful. However, what was missed by myself with many years of sober time is the simple fact that my flawed thinking which results in insane, mad decisions can reoccur at any time. My flawed thinking is a forever thing.

With hindsight, of course, I can see all the moves I made in my journey that spiralled towards disaster. I can see the mad decisions that were made with the best of intentions, the mad thinking and decisions that I asked nobody about. I did not check out my plans with anyone, I did not ask for input or help, or ask "do you think this is a good idea?" I was convinced at every crossroads that I knew what was best for me. I "told" people what I was doing, nothing was secret, however, I could not have been stopped at any time in the story towards disaster. Herein lies the answer for me, my arrogance returned, my self-will which has always been phenomenally strong returned, and was being directed not by the programme but by addiction.

I can see now that a decision to leave my home and country when still in the throes of grief was absurd, I can see that not researching the next place of work was mad, I can see jumping from the fat to the fire when I decided to go into business with a stranger was insane. I see it all today but did not, could not at the time. Because I did not see it and because I did not "work" the steps and check out my plans with others I have paid a huge price. No, I did not pick up drugs or alcohol, and for this, I am truly grateful. Others who make similar bad choices are not so lucky. My strong will does not allow me to get lost in the throes of substance abuse again, I have a very strong belief that it cannot be my answer any more. But I also believe things happen for a reason, perhaps to gain more understanding about this deadly disease. To be able to put down on paper more explanations of why and how the disease persists. To dispel those naysayers that still today talk about how addiction is not a disease and just a matter of choice. Those who believe it to be a choice cannot for one moment understand the theory behind flawed thinking and how this persists whether we drink or use or not. Research and science now tell us many things that were once unknown. Is it nature or nurture is a question often asked. To try to understand this disease in self, we all must look at our histories. All are different some are catastrophic, some are fabulous, all I can do is look at and tell about mine in the context of "Is life better?

Exercise One:

Flawed thinking which powers flawed decisions is the insanity talked about in Step two. When in this state I cannot see it, therefore I need to be able to check out my thought processes with others. Step three asks me to decide to do this. Check out my thinking, my plans, my ideas with others. This is another one of those things that sounds so easy to say yet is so hard to do and to continue doing. Could you do it? How does it feel? This is an exercise in ego deflation. It is the hardest of all the steps to achieve and keep on achieving. Primarily because of the addict's strong ego, and strong will-power. These things if kept in check can be wonderful assets, but in an egotistical, out of control addict, they can be the drivers toward destruction. The mad thing though is that the addict cannot see they are in flawed thinking when they are in flawed thinking. Only another person can/could help at a time like this.

8: Life as a Disaster Movie
(and how the wires become twisted)

Why do people become addicted? Is it nature, is it nurture? A question asked repeatedly. Is it bad breaks? Is it selfishness? Is it to escape? A million and one questions really about the nature of addiction. There is much research going on that enables us to look at these questions and come up with some new answers. Research that is looking at the brains of addicts and coming up with proof positive that the brains of addicts are different. Genetics play a part, as do the way life evolves for individuals. Addicts' brains are wired differently and create something that can be described as 'flawed thinking'. My thinking mechanism is different from others who are not addicted. Why does this happen? For a long time now, I have believed my life to resemble a 'disaster movie' with a start to life that many kids today also have, so, I know it cannot be unique, but while the 'twisted wires' concept goes some way in explaining some of my actions. Nature or nurture? It is difficult to decide in the ensuing tale.

I was conceived in Germany to unmarried German parents. My mother looking for an escape from the war-ravaged country of her birth, met an English soldier, who offered her a way out. England the land of daffodils and milk and honey. She left Germany with me as a secret passenger to settle in a land that did not like her accent.

She was strong and brave however and loved me and my siblings. He was a man who liked to drink. Was he an alcoholic? I think so but cannot say with any certainty as he never did. As a child, I was frightened of him and his rages when drinking, but I was still devastated when he left to be with another family that he liked better than ours. By that time, I had been told he was not my 'real' father. "I don't care", I thought, "I still love you, I don't care that you're not my real dad, "don't go" I stopped crying, held my breath - but he went anyway. I, and maybe everyone, holds their breath in times of stress, I still do it today hoping I guess to keep the pain away. It comes none-the-less.

My mother, the brave foreign warrior worked hard, kept us safe, and we flourished. We were damaged of course; broken homes will do this to you. As I grew, my shattering beginning showed in a shattered self-esteem. I was such a fearful girl. Blushed as you spoke to her. To find alcohol and other substances was altogether expected, it made a conversationalist out of me, I imagined it made me fun to be around. It took my social phobia and flipped it on its head. It taught me lots but much of it wrong. That I have no sense of belonging, no roots are perhaps inevitable. I tried, to have the same sort of life that I saw others live. Addiction, however, claimed me early on. As well as the usual bad behaviour and hangovers I developed traits such as 'geographicals'. I would move from place to place like a gypsy, like a nomad. Looking to find a place to be. I have lived in several different countries, several different towns looking always for a place to fit in. I have looked for 'better' all my life, so the question 'Is life better?' is seriously difficult for me to answer. I do know that had I continued to drink and drug and live the addict life I would not have survived it for very much longer.

Now not every addict has that sort of start to life, some people have fabulous everythings, and still end up in the same depths of despair, so it cannot just be circumstance that dictates who gets this illness. There are however many young people in our world today who are experiencing similar sorts of starts to life, or worse. If they have the genetic makeup which is then coupled with the unrest many of the displaced people of the world endure, I cannot help but fear that for generations to come the disease of addiction is going to have a field day. If the situation and public perception about addiction and what to do about it does not change, the already catastrophic statistics of deaths by addiction will only continue to rise.

As someone who works with addicts daily, this statistic is truly a devastating prospect, for this illness is eminently treatable. We should return to a former question about why on earth do we argue about how to treat it when there is a proven way already established? In the 1930s there really was nothing for the alcoholic or addicted person, institutions, prisons and madness or the streets were the choices for people like me. Two American men, a broker and a GP, both alcoholics, both down on their luck met and in that meeting were able to devise a plan, a system, something that has gone on to help millions of hopeless, addicted people. The Anonymous movement is very strong. It has survived without any government or private investment. It defies the myths and misconceptions that abound about it. It survives and grows and saves countless lives. It could do much more if it were viewed in the right way. If it were for instance not touted by some ignorant people as a cult or religion. Some religious people, of course, attend the meetings but so do countless others with no religion. This way of getting and staying free from addiction is truly remarkable. The anonymous part of the organisation is important to protect the shamed and frightened person who is looking for help. But it should not be invisible or unattainable to the world. It isn't completely of course because the desperate still find its rooms and walk into recovery, yet many do not, precisely because of the detractors who cannot accept that addiction could possibly be an illness, it is seen as a choice made by pathetic selfish individuals who choose to do this to themselves. This view keeps many away, too shamed to walk the path of recovery, too cowed by ignorance and prejudice. How on earth in the twenty-first century can this thinking still exist?

Without those two men in the 1930's who met and set the world of addiction on fire, I hate to think about where I might be. If not already physically dead, then certainly dying morally, emotionally and spiritually. Addiction does not claim our lives in nice clean sweeps but does it in the most degrading or humiliating of ways. On the way to death, we experience hundreds of little deaths, and what is even worse we take the people we say we love along for the ride. It cripples us by degrees, and as the disease progresses in us we fail in every way imaginable.

As already pointed out, one of the many reasons that people will not get help from AA is that little word God, which is in most of the literature that accompanies the fellowship. If people could suspend their fear or prejudice for even a little they might just find that what is asked of them in the meetings is to develop a 'spiritual awareness and to develop 'open minds'. Many people in adulthood if not earlier, start to develop a curiosity about the big questions about who we are, what is the world really all about and many other things. Some go on spiritual quests or journeys to find answers and there are lots of methods to helping in these journeys, even dare I say it people who believe they have/can find enlightenment as the result of ingesting some mind-altering substance or other. I tried LSD and 'magic' mushrooms several times in my early teens in a desire for enlightenment. I had read about others who had, it seemed, found wonderful places for their minds to go, had answers to some of the more spiritual questions about self and the world. Unfortunately, these lofty things escaped me, I found spiders and fear, I hated what my mind conjured up, it scared me witless. My darling brother who early in his using life, loved LSD at first, had a near-death experience on it which frightened him so much he refused to take it again. Yes, maybe we did not have the right kind of teacher or mind to attain enlightenment using LSD or mushrooms, but these experiences and many more that I have heard about since have convinced me it is not the path for me. I have discovered instead, that the 12-step programme not only assists in keeping me clean and sober but also takes me on a journey of sorts into myself, it enables me to examine and eradicate traits that no longer work for me or keep me in pain and enables me to develop traits any sage would be happy to possess. It takes hard and persistent work to change some of the self- defeating behaviours that have grown stronger in our addictions. For us addicts, there is no simple taking of a substance to attain nirvana, this is a fantasy, and many addicts have followed it to the gates of insanity or even death.

Enlightenment – understanding, awareness, wisdom, education, learning, knowledge, illumination, awakening, teaching, open-mindedness.

All explanations and words found in the Concise Oxford Dictionary

9: Let's talk about alcohol

Alcohol was the first drug I tried, for all the reasons everyone tries it, socially acceptable, reasonably priced even for teenagers. It seemed to be my 'go to' for just about every social situation. As a teen I liked to party, my social phobia, however, got in the way of any meaningful inroads to meeting the opposite sex, so a few drinks certainly made this avenue much easier to traverse. My drinking followed familiar patterns to many peoples. All so very normal until it wasn't. The dreaded blackouts occurred very early on in my drinking life, they terrified me, so I discovered some very dangerous ways to 'manage' them. More on this later as alcohol is the theme of this chapter.

Alcohol may have become ingrained in the social fabric of our lives, but it is far from a benign substance. The World Health Organisation (WHO) has stated that if it were discovered today it would be a banned substance. They go onto qualify this statement by saying that alcohol is a causal factor in more than 200 disease and injury conditions. Stunning statement!

The government recommendations for safe levels of drinking were **14 units** per person per week, (not night), **per week!** There are statements recently talked about on the main channel news that the latest NICE guidelines are now saying that NO alcohol is safe!

However:

Let's Talk About Units

The government recommendations for safe consumption of alcohol used to be 14 units per week for the average person.

How does this look?

1 Bottle of wine = 10 units

1 Glass of wine = 3 units

1 Pint of medium strength beer = 3 units

———————

14 units looks like:

14 single measures of spirit

7 pints of beer

7 glasses of wine

Units and safe recommendations are not even considered in the life of a regular heavy consumer of alcohol. It is not unusual to drink those 14 units and more every night, or for as long as the particular binge lasts. The latest recommendations will not be considered by addicts.

In addition to the serious acute effects of drinking more than the recommended limit on a regular basis, effects such as accidents, injury or alcohol poisoning will be seen regularly in ER rooms across the country. Prolonged alcohol consumption can also lead to a huge range of physical and mental health conditions, including damage to the body's internal organs. Here are just some of the things that can go wrong.

LIVER

Problems with the liver are perhaps the most well-known effects of alcohol abuse. As most of the alcohol is metabolised in the liver, heavy use can lead to damage such as inflammation and scarring which can lead to cirrhosis. The liver is, however, quite a resilient organ and symptoms of damage do not generally manifest until at an advanced stage.

PERIPHERAL NEUROPATHY

There is damage to nerve endings which usually affects the hands or feet so that the sufferer experiences pain or numbness which in turn affects walking or everything we use our hands and feet for. Sufferers can often be seen to be walking gingerly as they no longer 'feel' the ground as they walk.

PANCREAS

Drinking too much can also cause the pancreas to become inflamed, and both acute, (short term) and chronic pancreatitis can occur.

HYPERTENSION

High blood pressure which is a risk factor in heart attacks and heart failure are common problems caused through high alcohol consumption. As well as problems with the heart it can also be a causal factor for strokes, aneurysms and other serious physical conditions

MENTAL HEALTH

People often use alcohol to cope with anxiety, panic attacks, depression and other ailments. However long-term use of alcohol to cope with these issues usually increase the severity of these problems. Although the euphoric phase of drinking is what pulls people into its sway, this tends to be short-lived and the self-medicating aspect of drinking becomes akin to the scorpion with a deadly sting in its tail. When the chemistry of the brain as described in previous chapters becomes affected, dependence on this drug means that escape from its clutches can only be achieved with help. Denial of the problem usually accompanies the developing dependency. So, the user becomes trapped and blind to the problem, usually believing that drinking relieves the stress, depression or whatever is wrong and continuing to use seemingly without care. A brain that is in denial mode cannot care, it cannot see what everyone else can see.

BRAIN DAMAGE

Long term heavy drinking can lead to all sorts of brain-related issues. Dementia being the most well known and feared. Alcohol-related brain damage includes such things as Korsakoff syndrome which is where the brain has become so damaged that it renders the sufferer helpless and dependant on others. There are less severe things such as impaired memory or thinking all are avoidable, some improve if abstinence can be achieved, but some do not.

DIGESTIVE PROBLEMS – VITAMIN DEFICIENCY

Inflammation in the stomach lining causes gastritis, Acid reflux can be a re-occurring problem as can ulcers. All kinds of malabsorption problems occur creating all kinds of vitamin deficiencies. Abstinence from alcohol and doses of high potency vitamin B injections are regularly used to help with some of these symptoms. High doses of vitamin B and or Pabranex injections also helps with the suspected brain confusion or damage that occurs in heavy alcohol use, if the damage is not too pronounced.

ALCOHOL POISONING

A potential lethal condition is created when someone consumes a dangerous quantity of alcohol, binge drinkers usually are the worst affected by this. It can lead to choking on a person's own vomit, heart attacks and seizures.

STILL THINK IT IS BENIGN?

So, the view that somehow alcohol is a benign social lubricant is somewhat at odds with these horrible things that sometimes go wrong for the legendary heavy drinker. There are many more alcohol-related symptoms known to all who work in the field of addiction. The saddest perhaps are the people who become so depressed that suicide looks to be the only answer. Many many alcoholics who have failed to heed the warning signs in the downward progression of their illness have made plans to die or have attempted suicide. Life looks so bleak and impossible that the only way out is to end the pain permanently. We have met many in treatment who come close to making this irreversible decision. We talk to them about suicide being a permanent solution to a temporary problem. Sometimes treatment and abstinence change this type of thinking, but once those mental pathways are created in the brain, an individual will remain at risk from dangerous thoughts and must have help to cope. (More about this in later chapters)

MIXING SUBSTANCES

My solution to the dreaded blackouts that heavy drinking caused in myself, was to mix alcohol with other substances, mainly amphetamines or cocaine. The combination enabled me to drink without blacking out. The toxic effects of combining these substances were of course highly dangerous and could have resulted in many types of illness had I continued to abuse my body in this way. As it was I believe the progression of the illness in myself was accelerated, and I reached that point of misery and despair that heralded my rock bottom because of this acceleration. I am grateful today that I was able to see and partially understand what was going on, I am grateful I was able to accept the help that I needed. Many do not, they reach this same terrible place, where to go on means certain disaster yet for some inexplicable reason they will not stop, accept direction and turn away from disaster. Perhaps they do not see it, perhaps they do not believe it is as bad as all of that, perhaps they still believe *'just one more will not hurt.'*

So, this last sentence brings me full circle, 'let's talk about alcohol.' It must lose its benign status, people need to be educated on the dangers. We cannot go on ignoring this danger. All substances have equal danger status. Addiction is the thing that makes the substance a problem. For the percentage of people who become addicted, it does not matter if the thing causing the problems is illegal or can be bought in supermarkets and garages and found in everyone's homes. The only solution is to educate and make treatment available to all. Can we ever eradicate addiction? I do not think this could be easily achieved, but if we could reduce the shame and the stigma that addiction creates alongside it, then maybe we could have a society that reduces the deaths created by this illness and signposts people toward the right kind of help when help is needed.

10: What to do to get well?

In contemplating the heading of this chapter, the simple answer, of course, is everything possible. What exactly to do will depend on several different factors. The first being severity of your physical state. As already discussed the progression of the illness is a deciding factor for many of the choices you need to consider. Denial will have been broken enough for the sick addict to contemplate asking for help. There are different ways to access this help. Recovery from any addiction always starts with the need to stop using, as this is a fearful idea to most practising addicts, most need help to begin this process. It is also dangerous for some.

Depending on the severity and the progression of the illness, a detox is usually required. This is the most dangerous time for any addict as the withdrawal state can have severe consequences on the body. Proceeding with medical help is advised in the more severe cases.

But imagining that the individual is fit enough to endure treatment then the differences in all the choices at their disposal can be contemplated. There are lots of ways to access help, here are some of them:

- **Attending Counselling sessions.**
- **Going to a Treatment Centre**
- **Asking for help from your GP**
- **Local Drug and Alcohol Services in your area**
- **Going to a 12-step meeting**

What is Counselling?

There are many ways to describe counselling and many different types of counsellors. In contemplating what type of counsellor you need, generally, they will specialise in a field and have accompanying qualifications. My speciality, for instance, is addictions and I hold qualifications (NCAC) in this from the Federation of Alcohol and Drug Professionals (FDAP). I also practice Emotional Freedom Technique (EFT) and hold accreditation in this area. Other counsellors will be BAC accredited, and there are many more. Whomever you choose should have the relevant qualifications and be suitable for your issues.

There are many ways to describe what happens in a therapy session, but to keep things simple I will describe it as a process that enables one to look at what is contributing to your, worries, stress, ill-health or problem. It encourages people to look at and talk about aspects of their lives that do not seem to be working, and suggests changes in behaviour, feeling and attitude and how to do this. It can elicit changes in perceptions which in turn enable an individual to find new solutions to old problems.

A contract is usually entered for at least 6 sessions, more if necessary. Most counsellors do an assessment with you to determine the exact issues and to explain what needs to be done.

Sessions explore the problem in depth. You talk about events and reach the feelings that are holding you in pain. A variety of techniques will be used to help in this process

You talk about how to change and ways to make this happen.

You receive support and encouragement and look at what may derail or sabotage your progress. You also look at what support you may need to go forward.

Not all counsellors subscribe to an abstinence-based 12-step way of recovery. It is best to keep an open mind about all forms of help, as all forms of help are important as we look for sound Mental Health.

Treatment Centres or Rehab

In most treatment centres patients will have access to doctor's nurses and therapists, so all the things previously discussed will be available. Patients live in the clinic and contact with the outside world will be restricted. How this is managed is different for every centre. Some have very strict routines, and some are more relaxed. Addicts are all different and so are the treatment centres.

When Patients are physically able they will be invited into groups. Many people fear this concept and hope for one to ones as described in the counselling section previously. However, group work is exceptionally beneficial, fast and effective in treating addictions. Despite much fear when new, the newcomer is welcomed by people who know exactly how they feel, and the first-day fears are quickly extinguished. Patients learn from each other as well as therapists. Most rehabs have a strong educational push and patients learn about the disease of addiction. Perhaps for the first time, they begin to talk openly and honestly about the things they have done under the influence.

The feelings that accompany these experiences are what the therapists are encouraging from the patient, it can feel awful breaking down in tears or screaming in rage, or shaking in fear when describing an out of control life, but all these states and more are what keep the addict locked into self-defeating behaviours. This may sound extreme, but it is exactly this extreme emotional behaviour which makes rehab such a good choice to start recovery. It would be almost impossible to do this deep psychological work outside of a clinic, as well as holding down jobs, looking after families etc. Most people feel a huge sense of relief throughout their stays in rehab. A lot of psychological work is done, as well as ways to change and new practices to adopt. There are different areas of concern and growth for everyone, this is not a one size fits all by any means Rehabs also introduce their patients to a vast number of sober/clean ex-clients. People who are exhibiting the new behaviours which are currently being taught. Patients will also be introduced to the 12-step fellowship. A lot of changes need to take place to succeed in recovery, treatment centres begin this work with their patients. The 12-step fellowship and Aftercare in the clinic will be suggested to continue this work once treatment is finished. Family support and therapy is another aspect that will be looked at in treatment. It is rare for there not to be problems in the families of people who come to treatment.

There are different lengths of stay depending on what rehab you go to and what treatment package is chosen. This will be decided by you and whomever you speak to right at the start. We always recommend patients stay as long as possible because no matter how long they stay be it for a 7 day only detox, or a full programme (28 days or longer) it will never be enough time. An attitude that sees recovery as an on-going process will be encouraged. Addicts will never be cured, but life can get better, individuals can feel better, life can change and the downward trajectory of untreated addiction, reverses and goes the other way in recovery.

> **"Your vision will become clear**
> **Only when you can look**
> **Into your own heart.**
> **Who looks outside dreams,**
> **Who looks inside awakes"**
>
> *— Carl Jung*

11: Recovery

"The waking up" process as described by Carl Jung in the previous chapter is the process of recovery. Just about every addict is frightened by the prospect of either going to a fellowship meeting or by coming into treatment. Both have equal fear factors. As already stated the fear will continue in our society if the present attitudes about addiction prevail. Fear and shame are the things that keep most people away from accessing the help they need. If fear and shame surround this illness, the denial that serves the addict's mind so well will continue to exert its power over them, and consequently over our 'modern' society.

In treatment and in meetings the first thing to be addressed is the fear and the shame. When addicts hear others talking freely about their own shame and transgressions it is quite remarkable how much this changes fear. When newcomers see and hear that others have escaped the clutches of this disease, it starts an opening of the mind. When the mind begins to open, the facts about the disease can then penetrate. Once people realise that what is wrong are the symptoms of an illness and NOT a moral failing, well those are the moments that are well worth savouring. It takes time, however, to get this far. To get to this moment abstinence must be achieved, and this is easier said than done. Withdrawals both physical and emotional are hard things to tolerate. Sometimes dangerous, always uncomfortable. A medicated withdrawal is sometimes recommended, but as this can only be done with a doctor, this can be hard to access, because of many awful stories of detox medications being misused, GPs are sometimes loath to give them to people to detox at home. Speciality clinics can prescribe them, but medications for home detoxes are hard to access these days. A detox must commence and the duration of this will be determined by one's physical damage and level of physical dependence whilst using. The body can often take much abuse, but once that tipping point has been reached then catastrophic things may occur. Medical monitoring is always the best option.

The first few weeks will be uncomfortable no matter how far down the progression chart one has fallen. If not physical symptoms, then most definitely emotional symptoms will be rearing their uncomfortable head. This means that individuals will be tearful, or unhappy, or depressed, or sick, or angry or anxious. Or all these things. They may be unable to sleep properly, to eat right, or have any kinds of boundaries. They will resemble, just hatched chooks, unsteady and skittish, not so cute in some cases, but you get the idea! A huge amount of information must be collated and quickly if they are to survive the first weeks of attempting to get clean. Some can do it, others cannot. Recovery requires a lot of encouragement, kindness and understanding. At fellowship meetings, this is provided along with cups of tea, advice and support by the older more established members of the fellowship. In treatment, this is provided by staff dedicated to the treating of the illness, as well as peers who have been in situ a little longer. And understand the feelings and symptoms.

A lovely little poem written by **Guillaume Apollinaire** sums this up well.

> **"Come to the edge" he said,**
> **They said, "we're afraid".**
> **"Come to the edge" he said,**
> **They came, he pushed them**
> **And they flew**

Anyone who works with addicts understands the fear factors involved in making those hesitant steps towards recovery. Everyone understands the madness that accompanies this illness. Some of the people who want or need help are less than grateful, some are pretty combative. They want nothing more than to prove everyone wrong and some of them will fight and be obnoxious and blame everyone else and the world for the predicament they find themselves in. I have met some less than grateful individuals, I have been sworn at, and insulted, I have been trolled on the internet, (this is a new phenomenon) I have had letters of complaint written about me, all because I have chosen to do battle with this vile illness. When trying to treat the illness and the flawed thinking, individuals must be challenged. An addiction therapist can be neither soft nor a pushover, so for some this looks like a challenge too far. Most addicts don't like to be challenged. When the addict does not really want to change or wants to go on using then anything will be the excuse as to why treatment/meetings do not work. Arguing and blaming therapists becomes the sport at which these emotional vampires love to win. So why do we therapists and others who work with addicts do it? Because the benefits far outweigh the few who remain sick and unchanged. The benefits are of course when someone does find recovery, when someone who perhaps has been inches from ending their own lives is stopped and shown that suicide does not need to happen. When someone's family thanks us for helping get their loved one back into the family and the family is changed. Yes, these are the things that make working with addicts so rewarding. Experiencing the other stuff, however, reminds me how necessary it is to stay connected to the programme and work on self to change self. So far, I have only discussed coming into treatment, and the first three steps but much more work needs to be done to remain well.

What Next?

Surrender, admitting and accepting, finding help, accessing that help – the first three steps. There are twelve steps and each of them takes one to another part of the journey of restitution. To complete this journey, just like most journeys really, one needs a guide or two or three, in the fellowship meetings they take on the form of sponsorship, nothing to do with finances or money, but someone to help translate the further steps.

Step Four

Made a searching and fearless moral inventory of ourselves.

This step is often viewed with abject fear by newcomers. Why wouldn't it? Knowing the behaviours that addicts get up to in the active stages of the disease and finding out it must be examined and questioned is a terrifying thought at first. However, more experienced members of the 12-step movement will have more edifying thoughts about this process. When written out and done as instructed, what is discovered are traits which most humans have, but in addicts become some of the drivers for the more dangerous or self-defeating behaviours. If these character defects continue unchecked, then the addict will become unhappy, miserable and most likely blame it on recovery (or rather not using) If this occurs, it is not hard to see how a return to using happens. Along with the discovery of these traits, solutions are also found. They need to be worked on and remembered, our character defects or traits are rarely eradicated, just tamed and kept subdued, (a little like the sleeping tiger). The theory is that when and if they raise their troublesome heads the addict will understand what is driving the behaviour or feeling and be able to take the appropriate action to change them. We usually discover we have been angry and resentful about and towards the world and ourselves. The process of change offers us a way of resolving and healing some of this. In fact, it is crucial that we do. The founder of the 12-step movement has written *"anger and resentment are the number one reason for relapse" Bill W.*

Step Five

Admitted to God, to ourselves, and to another human being the exact nature of our wrongs.

We have to work with others when we discover what is revealed in the previous step. We often need help with this as some of the discoveries are awful. We can easily misunderstand and will need to reframe what we think and feel. We can get some of the discoveries wrong. Whatever happens, we cannot proceed alone in this confusing place, others are needed to direct and clear the way.

Angie C - Sobriety date 9/02/1981 - STEPS FOUR AND FIVE

My addiction to alcohol and drugs is my disease: what I did and shouldn't have and often didn't do and should have done as a result of my drinking and drugging; has left in its wake damage to others and self, causing guilt, shame, fear, anger and a shambles of a life.

In recovery it is my responsibility to change – through the first step, I accept the illness, in Step two and three I realise I cannot do this alone or change or fully understand how to change by myself.

Leading to Steps four and five.

A sincere (impossible to me in my using) and searching inventory of my self and actions. Leaving 'no stone unturned' and keeping no secrets.

Having written all this down, stripping away all the hiding, leaves me with a devastating galaxy of isolation, self-disgust and self-loathing, with the dread and expectation of revulsion, punishment, banishment and exile, instead, I received a *'me too'*, with a smile of unconditional love and acceptance.

What I looked for so avidly in the bottomless bottle and endless drugs was found. I am no longer alone, as I continue this journey with others in the fellowship of the spirit.

Step 6

Were entirely ready to have God remove all these defects of character.

Step 7

Humbly asked Him to remove our shortcomings.

These steps are simply instructions to change using the help that is available. We talk about how and what needs to change, we do not just let things fester and develop and get worse. Our sobriety depends on action to change some of our more deviant behaviours. If we don't, we suffer without the balm of a substance, if we don't change we are more likely to relapse.

K D - Sobriety Date: 16/05/2013 - STEPS SIX AND SEVEN

When I arrived in AA I was completely broken, full of fear, self-pity and depression. I could see no hope for the future. The only friend I had left was alcohol, and even this stopped working, it made no difference to the pain if I drank or not. Today I appreciate that to do Steps Six & Seven I needed to do the first five with a sponsor. I needed to admit and accept that I am powerless over my illness and could not change on my own. I had to gain an understanding about resentments and character defects and how they impacted and affected my behaviour. I also learned that this programme was spiritual and not religious, which was a relief as I did not believe in a religious God.

I was more than willing to be free of all my resentments and secrets, that I was able to reveal to my sponsor in Step Five. I understand today that these were some of the things I used to drink on and if they were not worked on could very well be the excuse to use again. I felt so humiliated by my behaviour, so had to find some peace with this feeling. Today I accept that I do not control or know everything and that there are 'others' who can and would help me. Steps Six & Seven continues to give me the opportunity to change and become a better version of myself today.

Step Eight

Made a list of all People we had harmed and became willing to make amends to them all.

Step Nine

Made direct amends to such people

wherever possible, except when to do so would injure them or others.

These steps are known as the amends steps, this is where we find out just who we need to make amends to. It is different to "I'm sorry". Amends are an acknowledgement of wrongs we have done to others and abstinence is the beginning of being able to change some of those wrongs. We may need to make direct amends, but these should always be done with the help of other longer sober individuals. If a newly sober addict just goes off to make amends for some wrongdoing without careful thought or discussion, a worse transgression can be made, the person being made the amend to may not understand, may be hurt more deeply than is realised and may not want your amend and then retaliate, anything can happen in these amends, so, proceed with caution. They do have to be done, but just carefully and with help. If they are done the sense of relief and growth can be enormous.

JoJo : Sobriety Date - 08/01/2013 - STEPS EIGHT AND NINE

Steps Eight & Nine focus on the continuing journey of examining ourselves and removing or correcting the things that no longer work. We identify those people we have had a negative impact upon and attempt to make amends. As we work these two steps, our emerging clarity allows us to first make a list of people we may have harmed in our using years. It is like unpicking the tangled knotted and ragged ugly tapestry that we have woven. We cannot eradicate those threads entirely; the shadow of that harsh weave will remain. But what we can humanly do is by careful unpicking and repairing, create a canvas for a new, rich and beautiful tapestry, woven by careful skill and design and love. The tapestry will form the lasting legacy of our own personal development and continued commitment to recovery as well as the foundation for loving, functional relationships. Step eight requires the creation of a list of those we have harmed. A daunting task which needs help to achieve. We work with conviction and courage. 'Courage' is a beautiful word – derived from the French Coeur – heart.

Step 9 requires prayer and meditation, the qualities of care, prudence, understanding and congruence. It is

not about scattering the confetti of 'apologies'. It is the gentle yet fearless, deep meaningful progression to the healing effect of making amends.

Step Ten

Continued to personal inventory and when we were wrong promptly admitted it.

This step is a reminder to continue to assess ourselves and an acknowledgement that we may never become saintly as we can often make mistakes. The antidote is to recognise them and do something about them. Admitting it to ourselves and others is a way of them not getting out of hand. It's rather a comforting step in a way as I would not like to be considered saintly.

Lizzie B – Sobriety Date 8/04/2016 – Step Ten

This step is an important one for me to make continued progress in my recovery. Putting the substance down was the relatively easy part, living life on life's terms takes effort, time and support. By using what I have learnt I can achieve a life in sobriety far more valuable, happy and fulfilled than life in unchecked addiction ever was. Step ten actions are an integral part of my daily routine, enabling me to live this sober life. My routine, begun in rehab, reaffirms who I am and what this means to me. 'I am an alcoholic and I won't take a drink today' I plan each day and then seek the courage, strength and guidance to achieve a positive day. For this to be successful I need to be aware of my strengths and weaknesses and be ready to communicate them with and to my support network. At the end of each day, I review how things went, what went well and what didn't. How can I improve outcomes and do I owe anyone an apology or amend? I also aim to have the willingness to accept that sometimes I will not meet the expectations of myself or others, but I understand it is 'progress not perfection' that I am aiming for. I can thereby achieve inner peace in a not always peaceful life.

Step Eleven

Sought through Prayer and meditation to improve our conscious contact with God *as we understood Him* praying only for knowledge of His will for us and the power to carry that out.

This step reminds us that this disease affects our spirit as well as everything else. Going back to Steps two and three we look at what we said here and ask ourselves what else needs doing. As we develop and grow, our spirit motivates and directs us in ways we could hardly imagine at the start of our journey. We read and study and talk to others about what Step eleven means to them.

Phil – Sobriety date 19/8/2017 - Step Eleven

Prayer and meditation – I have no control over when the God of my understanding chooses to influence my thinking. I remain actively open to the need for help and guidance. *Improve our conscious contact* – I do this whenever and wherever I want. I choose not to kneel and have had my most profound moments of "God Consciousness" while walking the dogs, while sitting on the edge of my bed and while queuing for a coffee. They have all been quite profound. *God as we understand Him* – It doesn't matter if I do or don't believe in God, so long as I know I am not it. I tried giving up alcohol using my will, it didn't work. The God of my understanding is not the God of my childhood, nor the God as depicted in scripture, but it is something 'outside of myself

Step 12

Having had a spiritual awakening as a result of these steps, we tried to carry this message to alcoholics and to practice these principals in all our affairs.

This step tells us that the preceding eleven steps have resulted in a *spiritual awakening*, to keep, to grow and develop this awakening, we need to carry the message. What is the message? The message is us, the message is that there is a way out of the hell of addiction. The message is if you do these things too, you can also find a way out.

It all may seem like a very tall order, but the promise of AA is that if you are simply willing to try to do some of these things you will find growth. You are looking for progress and not perfection.

Charlie M - Step Twelve

Step twelve for me is about sharing the message of recovery with others. It is what my recovery has given me and how I now live my recovery in every aspect of my life. Having gone through the journey of steps one – eleven I have been able to identify and accept my addiction. I have looked into and at myself and shared the results. I have looked into and at the effect I have on others and made amends as much as possible for this. So now in Step twelve I reap the benefits of this by having 'a life beyond my wildest dreams', one that is free of the shackles of addictive behaviour. Yes, the thoughts are still there, and the behaviour is always ready to try to entice me, however, I can now take my message of recovery to the outside world and share it with others at the meetings I attend. I talk to other addicts, 'do service' within the programme and realise that these types of behaviours need to be done in all parts of my life. Although I am an addict in recovery, I am not JUST an addict in recovery. So I practice these principles in all my daily life, this is what true and absolute living recovery is to me.

12: Relapse

Now wouldn't it just be hunky dory if everyone who stumbled upon some of the concepts spoken about, got themselves to meetings or rehab, did the work suggested and were able to live happily ever after? Yes, it would, however, the reality is not so marvellous. A big proportion of people who go to meetings or go to rehab will relapse again. This is the thing that makes no sense to anyone least of all the addict themselves. The reasons are multi-faceted, no one reason fits all. Some of the best relapse prevention information available talks about the idea of preparing for relapse!

Preparing for Relapse – PLAN

Rather than this being a negative idea, perhaps a change of thinking is also required to understand this. The truth of the matter is that many people can and do relapse, some very soon after hearing about the recovery programme through AA or through a rehab, and there are others who relapse again after, 10 days, 10 weeks, 10 months or ten years, and upwards, with all the numbers in-between! There is no cure for the illness, there is no complete and utter reversal of symptoms, once the line to addiction has been crossed then it is something that is there for life. Addicts must work hard at staying on the right side of the line, and the truth is they don't always do so. So, the only way to view this is to plan for relapse, which means:

If I relapse, this is what I will do

- I will ring someone for advice or help - my sponsor, the clinic, my therapist
- I will do what it takes to abstain again, I will cold turkey if it is safe, I will go to the doctor or back into the clinic for a detox
- I will do what I'm told! I will go to meetings and stop doing it my way
- I will not isolate, or be secretive, or tell lies
- I will fall in 'love' with recovery, in other words be interested, involved and pro-active in the recovery world and my new way of life

All these things and more will have to be achieved to get back on track, it is usually harder after a relapse, the sense of shame is greater. Sadly, some people never return from relapse, some die.

That is the reality of this illness. The result of a trajectory downwards is death.

There are other things that must be understood about the illness, recovery and relapse.

PAWS Post-Acute Withdrawal Syndrome

Most people understand about withdrawal symptoms, of course, we all know about the shakes, the sweats, the inability to sleep, the depression etc. However, what is not so well know is that these things are the acute symptoms. There is a whole mess of other things addicts must contend with at times. There are second stage withdrawal symptoms, which are more psychological and emotional than physical. They occur as the brain chemistry gradually returns to normal. As the brain improves the levels in the brain chemicals fluctuate creating PAWS. The symptoms are: mood swings, anxiety, irritability, tiredness, variable energy, low enthusiasm, poor or variable concentration and disturbed sleep. They will feel like another rollercoaster of sorts, with symptoms that can be changeable, they come and go, sometimes disappearing for days only to come back again. Good stretches of emotional health will get longer, but the bad periods feel bad. They can last a few hours or a few days. There are no obvious triggers, a person in recovery will just wake up one day with some of the symptoms and feel tired and restless. They will discover the symptoms can lift just as suddenly. Some people experience PAWS for up to 2 years. If it is remembered that they come, and they go and there is an end in sight, they can be survived. Patience and kindness, especially to self, are needed to work through these symptoms. All the resources learnt previously are needed to get and stay well. Lots of meetings, contact with others. Maybe some Yoga, and meditation, acupuncture or other alternative healing techniques. The idea behind some of the alternative methods of healing are to quieten the very stressed, noisy, chaotic internal lives. The worst thing to do is to isolate and hide away. All the things discussed in this segment, of course, can be a prelude to relapse. So, people need to know about it and know that a return to the substance of choice will do nothing except take one back to the beginning. Addicts must go through some of this, it is part of early recovery. Once they have learnt about PAW'S and the symptoms to beware of then they are ready to learn about the stages of relapse.

STAGES OF RELAPSE

Relapse trends to be a process and not an event. Some people who relapse will swear blind they do not know what went wrong and 'it just happened' We who work with the illness know this is far from the truth. The many relapses that we witness can often be traced back to one or several things not done or done. When looking at anyone's relapse we start to chart events and ask lots of questions. There are three distinct areas to look at:

Emotions, mental health, and physical signs.

Emotions

If you have read the chapter on PAW's you will have some idea of the emotional symptoms to look out for, as emotional relapse resembles this state.

Anxiety, intolerance, anger, defensiveness and mood swings, in fact, many of the symptoms that were always the reason to use in the past. Once the emotional discontent sets in, it may then follow well-worn paths of isolation and not asking for help, missing meetings or going to them late and leaving early so's not to have to talk to anyone. Other things start to break down too and you will see a return to poor sleeping habits, late nights and not getting up in the morning. If these are not recognised as possibly part of an emotional relapse things will continue to get worse, until the person experiencing this will want to escape, feel exhausted and emotional relapse then moves onto the next stage.

Mental Relapse

In this state, many people will be having strong urges to use again. There may be a fight going on internally as the old way of dealing with adversity attempts to gain dominance over new ways of behaviour. People, places and things you used with will start to take over your thinking. Glamorising the using and fantasising about the past will start to disrupt your life. Words like 'it was so much better when…' will convince you that it is sobriety and recovery that is the culprit in this saga. Hanging around old haunts and with old using friends herald the beginning of the end in this story. The last stage is:

Physical Relapse

Once the thinking starts to go this way then physical relapse is only a matter of time. At this stage, it will be very hard to stop relapse from happening. Holding onto recovery or abstinence for dear life is never a good way to achieve sobriety. It is painful and rarely works for long.

Solutions

In all the stages of relapse, there are different things that can be done to avert disaster.

Recognise that the emotional crisis you are in is serious and needs attention.

The best thing to do is to talk to someone about how you are feeling.

Practise self-care do some of the recovery things that you did in the beginning.

Meetings, yoga, meditation, early nights, timetabled days.

For the glamorising and fantasising there is a saying in the programme of **'play the whole tape'** in other words start to remember what happened at the end of a binge, not just the euphoria at the beginning. Remember the pain and trouble, remember the pain in your partner or children's eyes.

There is a very real need to work hard at recovery daily, simply becoming abstinent will not be enough. Abstinence is the start not the end to things, yet many people who relapse believe they have got 'better' because they have stopped using. The 12-step method of getting recovery takes one on a journey into the self. But the journey is continuous and never ends, if people struggle with any of the emotions or behaviours then it is a signal that something needs to be worked on. The biggest problem in any of the relapse situations that can occur is that the addict almost automatically isolates and does not talk about what is going wrong.

Communication and connection are so important in this recovery journey. There is a very real need to start building a support network, not just of meetings but of the people at the meetings who can help. To ask for help people need to learn to trust one another. Trust is a commodity that is precious. In active addiction, no-one is trustworthy, and nothing is trusted. So, it is a very new game entirely for addicts to begin to trust and be trusted. There may be a need to start building trust with a professional first, and as some of the deeper more devastating issues are talked about and processed, and when the person learns about the relief that is gained then trust becomes a whole lot easier, as well as something to be desired.

13: Anger and The Family

In the whole complex tale of addiction and recovery, the most amazing thing to happen for those in recovery is that after the stark, despairing, shameful moments that occur in seeing the truth about themselves when using, there emerges from these ashes a being that can love, live and laugh. In other words, after many years, of anaesthetising feelings, they begin to change and experience the full range of feelings again. However, this is a joy and a curse as along with the wonderful stuff there also comes the not so wonderful stuff. One of the most difficult and dangerous feelings for recovering people to try to deal with in recovery is anger. Perhaps it is the most difficult for everybody, but for the recovering addict it is essential that they get a handle on this emotion quickly, learn how to identify it and learn how to express it correctly, it is not too dramatic to say that their lives depend on it.

Some of the literature talks about **'anger and resentment being the reason for many of the relapses'**. Relapse, of course, is dangerous especially after a period of clean time, as it is easy to mistake how strongly the drug will affect the body. Most addicts understand anger to be **'a drink or drug under construction'** So with these kind of serious consequences, addicts in early recovery would be wise to do their homework on this emotion and learn how to deal with it appropriately.

Addiction is known as **'the angry disease'**, so from the get-go, addicts must be aware they are in for a bumpy ride. Everything about early sobriety is difficult and coming to their senses seems to bring everything to the surface in a rush. The jangled shredded nerves of someone who no longer uses are difficult to experience for the addict, but for everyone else too. The surrender process that starts in Step one begins with an acknowledgement of the worst of the using behaviour. Most addicts are furious with themselves, but also with the world at large. They have never adequately dealt with their feelings without first anaesthetising with a substance. Sometimes the anger comes when drunk or drugged too, but nine times out ten, the memory of feelings felt, and the behaviour gets swallowed up in blackout and many other issues that drunken 'out of it' behaviour creates. Shredded nerves cannot cope with normal life, everything can create frustration in the early days of getting clean. In treatment, we begin working with this feeling by first stating that **Anger is a Natural Human Emotion,** it is felt by everyone. **It is also called a Survival Mechanism.** It becomes **Destructive** or **Constructive** depending on how it is used. This is sometimes a revelation to the newly sober person and always a relief to think that everyone feels the feeling. The process of opening up and talking about how they feel is once again emphasised as being one of the more important things people must learn to do in recovery. **Addicts used on feelings. They used when happy, sad, frightened, ashamed.** Any feeling was a reason to use. Addicts have never learnt to process or use most feelings except destructively, and people around them are very often left to pick up the pieces of their shattered selves once the addict has unleashed the emotions either at them or the world. Addicts are good at the 'blame game' Everything wrong that occurs is someone or something else's fault. Learning that their feelings are their responsibility is quite liberating for the rest of the world, but very difficult for the addict. Early recovery certainly does not feel liberating sometimes, so the addict needs endless patience and understanding, from other addicts who are somewhat further on in the recovery process. To expect family and friends to be patient and understanding is sometimes too much. They too have their anger issues to deal with. (more about the family later).

Sadly, this emotion is a tough one for addicts to learn about. How to express it constructively is difficult, it takes time and very often goes wrong. We often recommend **Anger management groups or courses** for the very angry souls who cannot find an easy way through.

For family members and loved ones, they are the ones who usually bear the brunt of firstly the out of control behaviour and feelings including anger, of the practising addict, and then to add insult to injury they bear the brunt of an addict's emerging trials in early recovery. The newly sober person is not always the easiest to be around, and early recovery is hard for them but sometimes even harder for family members. Family members friends or loved ones can sometimes develop resentments of their own when the newly recovering addict starts to request that social life and things like alcohol in the home are all danger areas. "You have the problem, so why do I have to pay a price" is a refrain sometimes uttered. It is because it was recognised very early on in this story of recovery that if it were to succeed then the family members should also be helped to move past the destructive phase of addiction. Understanding the Disease Concept goes a long way in explaining why certain things are off-limits in early recovery. The 12-step movement has Al-Anon, Al-Ateen, Families Anonymous and CODA as the support mechanisms specifically for families. Most treatment Centres have family support groups, where things can be explained and eventually understood, and accepted. However, sometimes the problems within the home have been so destructive that to get to understanding is a tough road. Some relationships do not make it.

Angie Cullen – Family Therapist (RMN and NCAC - FDAP) writes:

Consequences get addicts into recovery, no consequences, no problem! Families and carers who love their addict want to care, protect and help them, which usually prevents or reduces the consequences. They often feel they are keeping the addict alive. This enables the addiction process to continue to progress. Just as the addict becomes obsessed with the using behaviour, "when can I next use, where will the money come from, how can I hide it and what excuses can I give"; the family member or loved one becomes obsessed with the addict. – "Where are they, surely, they had more than one, shall I call the hospitals, police, or friends?"

For the concerned and obsessed family's friends and loved ones the feelings surrounding all of this resembles that of the addiction itself. It is not unusual for wives and husbands, children too, as well as friends or concerned on-lookers, to feel they are going mad. For all these people what is required is an understanding of "The Disease Concept" – this information is pivotal in helping them recognize, accept and reduce feelings of anger, guilt and shame. They need to learn the benefits of detachment.

Some families have had years of being affected by living with the addict and addiction, it has at best, distorted good relationships. For relationships to survive, everyone needs to have an opportunity to talk and be listened to and supported. To understand what has been going on and to receive therapy if needed. Most family members and friends feel an enormous sense of relief when they realise they are not alone and there is help for them and their addict.

Detachment – neutrality, impartiality, disengagement, dispassion

RMN *– Registered Mental Health Nurse*

NCAC *– National Counsellor Accreditation Certification*

FDAP *- Federation of Drug and Alcohol Professionals*

14: Secondary Care

Most of what has already been talked about has concentrated on getting the sick addict into treatment, if they go to a rehab this is known as Primary treatment, where everything about the addiction is concentrated on to get the addict 'better' and able to function well enough to get on with life. For some individuals, this will not be enough time to resolve all the life difficulties, no matter how long they stay in the Treatment Centre. Let me now introduce you to the concept of Secondary Care.

Paul Baker, Programme Manager ANA Treatment Centres writes:

Some individuals who safely traverse Primary Treatment will recognise that when it is time to leave treatment that they do not have adequate support or structure to put into practice all they have learnt in primary treatment. Secondary treatment, therefore, affords an individual time and structure in which to put into practice what has been learnt. This consists of a 'managed' daily routine that includes attending open groups with other recovering people, workshops on all the diverse subjects needed to succeed with recovery. Some subjects would be:

- Exploring how all the 12-steps work together
- Relationship Education
- Co-dependency
- Love and addiction
- Intimacy in recovery
- Family roles and recovery
- Relapse Prevention
- Budgeting/Finances etc.
- Finding work

The aim in Secondary care is for the client to live semi-independently with other peers and to work on looking after the house they stay in as well as commuting to the centre daily. They will attend evening Fellowship meetings and will be encouraged to actively look for a sponsor and to widen their support network. They could attend the educational facilities in the local area and/or become volunteers within the community. On-going treatment in Secondary Care also encompasses key-work sessions with a focal counsellor as well as family conferences when required. Lots of work is usually required within family structures.

Secondary treatment is sometimes described as a bridge to normal living. This supported and structured way of living is an important bridge between Primary residential treatment and living within the community post-treatment. Secondary

programmes have usually been developed over many years and provide not only on-going treatment, but a collaborative relationship with the local community such as Colleges, sports facilities, volunteer opportunities, housing and relocation services as well as medical services.

There is much for the newly recovered individual to learn. Some have not lived 'normal' lives for many years, some have lost all connections to their family of origin, and some just need extra time to get used to sobriety and being clean.

Other things to consider

There are many Secondary Care facilities both in the UK and abroad. Some are gender specific, such as men or women only houses. Some focus on a specific type of lifestyles, such as the 'great outdoors', or country or town living. It will depend on what individuals are looking for going forward. Choosing the right place is, of course, important, so talking and asking lots of questions as in any new venture is encouraged. The goal in all the different aspects of treatment is to enable the individual whose life has been reduced to a hangover and despair to change direction and discover a different way of life.

15: Understanding Suicide and Addiction

In many of the stories encountered from recovering people, thoughts about suicide crops up more often than you would realise. Addicts often reach a point in their using lives when life looks bleak or empty, or they are filled with such shame and despair that to wonder if life is really worth living any more is often par for the course.

The rates of suicidal thoughts and behaviours are significantly higher among individuals with a mental disorder, addiction or both. Early recovery is not always a protection against feeling suicidal. As previously discussed, early recovery is sometimes when these feelings become strongest.

The isolation, secrecy and out of control feelings and behaviours are perhaps reasons why suicidal ideation is so prevalent amongst people with addictions. The feeling and idea that nothing can help, nothing can change "I will always feel like this" are strong reasons to feel that life is not worth it. Anxiety, depression, sadness, anger and shame, are all feelings which accompany addiction and early recovery. This is just another aspect of the insanity of the addicted mind, the twisted minds and logic of people who cannot see a way out of the hell created by their illness.

Powerlessness itself creates a desperate hopeless kind of state, powerlessness is what has to be acknowledged by every addict who wants recovery, it is not a pleasant feeling or state. It sometimes creates rage which if not checked brings on more denial. If not rage, then certainly shame and despair are often felt at this time. Owning up to and seeing what has happened as the addiction held dominance is frightening. If the individual who is going through this state is working with others they will find relief and even comfort from being supported and will gain understanding when told that this state or feeling is common and will not last forever. If they can stay abstinent, then with specific psychological work all of the feelings can change. Life can change.

Communication and Connection are so essential when striving for recovery, yet it is these two things that are so difficult for addicts to do.

A life of denial has had to be constructed to hide or 'get away' with intolerable behaviours. Isolation is the state preferred by someone with advanced addiction, it is easier to do what they want in isolation, yet it is exactly this that creates so much danger and misery for the person trying to get sober or clean.

The Mental Health of addicts, both whilst they are using but more so when the using stops, is very fragile. Once those hopeless feelings and thoughts 'life is not worth living' or 'I am useless, the world would be better off without me' start it is very difficult if not impossible to halt them alone. Without the substance which was used sometimes as a buffer to the slings and arrows of life, the addict has few resources at hand when left to their own devices to cope with and deal with their own thinking and feelings. Seeing life in 3D instead of rose tinted glasses takes a lot of adjusting to.

Many people who come into rehab talk of suicidal ideation, thinking about killing oneself, planning on how to do it and the actual doing of the act are distinct stages and different. It is important in therapy to discuss all of the manifestations of this kind of thinking and behaviour. People are sometimes fearful of talking about something like this, but it is in the talking about it that they will find relief and solace and recovery. It is difficult and scary and should be done with the help of professionals. If there is an underlying depression or other mental health problems, these will need to be treated as well as the addiction. Communication, therapy and medication are all used in these cases. The important message to leave this subject with is that whatever the feeling state of the individual there is a solution. Other people have walked this path before you and there is a way out no matter how black the road ahead looks.

16: Conclusion

To conclude I will return to one of the first questions I posed in this book. 'Is life better in Recovery?'

Sincerely and without a doubt, I can answer yes, it is. Heaven only knows I have had some very difficult things to negotiate in recovery, things like the death of loved ones, critical illness in self and others, redundancy and of course my on-going difficult situation which resulted in bankruptcy. I always say that more difficulties have assaulted me in my recovery than ever did whilst I was using. If I was so inclined I could use this one statement as the reason or excuse to pick up a nice mind-numbing substance and blank it all out! But thank heavens I have a little more sanity in my life today and can see that realistically that as we age and mature, life sometimes dishes out a plethora of difficulties that need to be dealt with. I understand today that my recovery means I have been given the gift of being able to deal with life on life's terms.

Some of us never 'grow up' and some of us feel that life 'shouldn't' be so hard. 'it's not fair' is a repeated refrain from young children and teenagers as well as early recovering addicts. Perhaps life is not fair but dealing with everything that life gives us with grace and dignity far outweighs the self-seeking piteous practising addict who continues to use life and misfortune as the excuse for not coping and needing to use the substance or addiction to cope. No single thing that can ever happen to us, will be made better by ingesting or indulging in an addictive behaviour or substance. The momentary relief is not worth the enduring pain it always brings. The fact that addicts continue to believe that solace will be found in addiction shows the insanity they live in. All of the literature pertaining to the 12-step philosophy talks about being restored in mind, body and soul. In other words, this is a long and complex journey, but one that brings us to an infinitely better place than the place addiction takes us to.

> **Are you searching for your soul?**
> **Then come out of your prison.**
> **Leave the stream and join the river**
> **that flows into the ocean.**
> **Absorbed in this world**
> **You've made it your burden.**
> **Rise above this world.**
> **There is another vision…**
>
> *– Rumi*

Resources

Alcoholics Anonymous (Big Book) - AA World Service

Addiction as a disease – David R. Hughes, 1997

www.medicalonline.com

www.mentalhelp.net

Pleasure Unwoven DVD Kevin Macauley

Memo To Self DVD – Kevin Macauley

The House I live in –DVD

That Sugar – DVD

I Want to Change my Life – Steven M. Melemis, PhD. MD

Chasing The Scream - Johann Hari

One Breath at a Time – Kevin Griffin

DSM – V – www.verywellmind.com

Quotes from:

Carl Jung – Rumi – Guillaume Apollinaire

Acknowledgements to...

All the brave contributors for the Step translations.

Some grateful thanks:

To Libby Reid and Mandy Harrison for their sterling support in editing and proofreading, advice and friendship.

Huge kudos go to Bill and Bob for saving my life, and for the fellowship that goes on saving millions of lives.

To Steve Stephens for helping me see my truth.

To Wendy Allenet-Simpson for the support at the start of this book when the world looked bleak. The beautiful beach house was a soul saver, thank you.

To Karen D, Charlie McAdam, Julie Stokes and Steve Pomeroy for being such amazing supporters of my quest to 'change perceptions one book at a time'.

Also by Sarina Wheatman

*Available worldwide from Amazon
and all good bookstores*

**Make an author very happy and leave an
Amazon Review – thank you!**

Contact Sarina Wheatman:

www.sarinawheatman.com

---

www.mtp.agency

www.facebook.com/mtp.agency

@mtp_agency

www.ingramcontent.com/pod-product-compliance
Lightning Source LLC
LaVergne TN
LVHW091555060526
838200LV00036B/849